Travel Agencies and Tourism Management

Travel Agencies and Tourism Management

B.S. Badan
Harish Bhatt

Commonwealth

Travel Agencies and Tourism Management

Edition : 2026

ISBN 81-311-0069-3

Published by :

COMMONWEALTH PUBLISHERS
4831/24, Prahlad Street,
Ansari Road, Darya Ganj,
New Delhi - 110002
Ph. : 23275511, 23257835
Fax : 91- 011- 23257835
e-mail : campusbooks@hotmail.com

Typesetting by :
Rishu Computers
Delhi

Printed at :
Roshan Offset Printers
Delhi

PREFACE

Tourism can be defined as the act of travel for the purpose of recreation, and the provision of services for this act. It is a service industry, comprising a number of tangible and intangible components. The tangible elements include transportation systems—air, rail, road, water and now, space; hospitality services, accommodation, foods and beverages, tours, souvenirs; and related services such as banking, insurance and safety and security. The intangible elements include: rest and relaxation, culture, escape, adventure, new and different experiences.

Travel and tourism is a major industry in the world and is at the top of the league of invisible earners of foreign currency. Many sovereignties, along with their respective countries and states, depend heavily upon travel expenditures by foreigners as a source of taxation and income for the enterprises that sell services to these travellers. Consequently the development of tourism is often a strategy employed either by a non-governmental organization or a governmental agency to promote a particular region for the purpose of increasing commerce through exporting goods and services to non-locals.

During recent years the tourism industry has witnessed unprecedented growth. Increasing consumer demand for educational and participatory travel experiences has resulted in a variety of specialty niche markets such as ecotourism, cultural-heritage tourism, and agritourism. New paradigms link strategic tourism planning with sustainable development.

The leisure and tourism industry is one of the leading global economic activities, a multi-billion-dollar industry with

700 million international travellers per year around the world. Tourism is a motor for employment and income creation and, especially in poor countries, a vehicle for development. But today it is not sufficient to simply create employment without regard for the quality of jobs and the social and environmental effects of tourism in vulnerable areas. A growing number of organizations, including the tourism industry leadership, are increasingly conscious of the risks and are adopting a more responsible attitude.

The present publication provides an authoritative look at how to manage travel and tourism industry in a better way. It introduces the complexities of the tourism system so that they will be better positioned to eventually assume the managerial challenges and responsibilities in a diverse and challenging industry. The latest advancements in tourism theory and thinking, retaining the thoroughness of content, diversity of applications, regional and international issues, economic significance, tourism operators and the role of technology in the tourism industry etc. are also described elaborately. Numerous regional and global case studies and examples are included to provide an appropriately broad geographic context. This work will be highly informative and useful to students, researchers, policy makers, managers and working groups of travel and tourism industry.

B.S. Badan
Harish Bhatt

CONTENTS

1
INTRODUCTION

Once a travel and tourism organisation has selected the most appropriate strategic options, the organisation must consider a number of key issues related to actually putting what is proposed into practice. As ever, the danger can lie in this more detailed level of strategic management. However, well thought out the strategy may be, if sufficient thought is not given to the ways in which it should be implemented it is unlikely to prove to be successful. In this section of the book a number of the most important issues connected with strategic implementation are considered.

First, implementation requires a reconfiguration of the travel and tourism organisation's resource base. Does the organisation have the inputs it needs in terms of finance, people, physical inputs and intellectual assets to carry out the strategy? If not these will have to be obtained.

Second, the travel and tourism organisation will need to bring its structure and culture into such a position that they facilitate a successful outcome. It may be that the structure and culture are not initially supportive for the strategic changes the organisation is trying to implement. In such a situation the organisation will need to instigate the requisite changes.

Third, implementation of strategy invariably involves change. This will affect employees' roles and responsibilities, may mean redundancies or additional appointments and external stakeholders such as shareholders will also be implicated. Change can be a difficult managerial challenge.

While some may welcome proposed changes others may resist, thus risking the efficient implementation of the strategy. Managers may adopt different approaches according to the circumstances.

Fourth, in an inherently international industry such as travel and tourism an important consideration is the approach of organisations to internationalisation. International strategy is considered.

It is likely that, following on from the four issues considered above, each functional area of the organisation (finance, marketing, human resources, operations, etc.) will need to consider implementing detailed strategies, which focus on each area of activity. This level of detail, however, is beyond the scope of this book.

The word 'implementation' perhaps implies that it is a 'one-off' process with the strategy being is implemented then left alone. This is not the case. Strategic management should be viewed as an on-going process, for lessons learned (both successes and failures) from the implementation stage can be fed back into the analysis phase. The external and internal environments of travel and tourism organisations are constantly changing so that such an organisation needs continually to re-evaluate its environments. Changes in these may require modifications to the chosen strategies and consequently revisions to the ways in which they are implemented.

At the end of a book on strategic management for travel and tourism it is apposite to stand back and consider the changing nature of the subject-matter.

2

STRATEGIC EVALUATION AND SELECTION

Introduction

Important decisions are never easy. In order to ensure that we make the right choice in any given situation, we must first of all be in possession of all relevant information. This is the purpose of the strategic analysis stage – to ensure that the management of a business is fully aware of the internal strengths and weaknesses, and of the external opportunities and threats.

The next stage in making an important decision is to be aware of *all* of the options available. The most obvious choice is not necessarily the right one. Following the generation of options, the next stage is to evaluate each option using consistently applied criteria. The purpose of evaluation is to ensure that all options are assessed with equal thoroughness. Finally, strategic selection involves actually making a decision based upon the evaluation of the options.

This chapter considers each of these stages in turn.

Learning Objectives

After studying this chapter, students should be able to:

- describe the nature of strategic options;
- explain the key areas that strategic decisions concern;
- describe the four criteria that are applied to strategic options;

- understand the financial tools that can be used to evaluate strategic options;
- understand a number of other tools that can be used to evaluate strategic options;
- understand a worked examples of the tools and techniques in relation to travel and tourism organisations;
- explain the limitations of an emergent approach to strategy when it comes to strategic evaluation and selection.

Identifying Strategic Options

The Nature of Strategic Options

At the start of this chapter, we must remind ourselves of what makes a decision *strategic* in nature as opposed to one that is *operational*.

Strategic decisions are taken at the highest level of an organisation. They concern decisions on how the whole organisation broken down into its constituent SBUs will be positioned in respect to its product and resource markets, its competitors and its macro influences. Accordingly, the options at the strategic level are those that offer solutions to the 'big questions' in this regard.

Operational level decisions are those that are concerned with how the internal parts of the organisation should be configured and managed so that they best achieve the strategic objectives.

The 'big questions' that are considered in strategic selection usually concern three major areas:

- Decisions on competitive strategy.
- Decisions on products and markets relating to the direction of development.
- Decisions on methods of development.

In most cases, an organisation will need to make continual decisions on all of these matters. We should not lose sight of the fact that the strategic process is just that – a process. Strategic selection is no more of a 'once for all' activity than either strategic analysis or strategic implementation. For organisations that exist in rapidly changing environments, decisions on strategic options will be required on a continual basis, hence the importance of ensuring we have a good grasp of the issues that are discussed in this chapter.

Competitive Strategy Decisions

Decisions over the organisation's competitive or generic strategy are important not only because they define the organisation's competitive position, but also because they will determine the way that the internal value chain activities are configured.

If the company elects to pursue a differentiation strategy, for example, the implications of this will be felt in all parts of the organisation. The culture and structure will need to be configured in such a way that they support the generic strategy and the product features and quality will also reflect it. Similarly, the way that the organisation sources and configures its resource base will need to support the strategy.

The same issues will be considered if a cost-driven strategy is chosen, although the way in which the internal activities are configured will be somewhat different.

Product and Market Decisions

The questions over *which products* and *which markets* are extremely important, because they can determine not only the levels of profitability but also the survival of the organisation itself. It is likely that strategy will involve a change in the SBU or company's size. If 'stability' is the chosen option this does not mean that nothing should be done, since to do so would invite competitors to enlarge their market shares. In such circumstances market share may be fiercely defended through such measures as pricing, promotional offers or increased levels of efficiency. Furthermore, even if the market share remains stable if the market as a whole is growing then the size of the overall business will increase, i.e. to use the analogy of a cake, one's slice of the cake may remain constant but the overall size of the cake is growing. If retrenchment is the chosen option decisions have to be made concerning which product or market areas should be reduced, sold off or withdrawn.

In cases where growth is the chosen strategic option that the organisation will pursue, decisions have to be taken about the direction of growth. These strategic choices arise from Igor Ansoff's (Ansoff, 1987) framework and should not be confused with Porter's generic strategies (Porter, 1985). Ansoff's generic growth strategies concern whether growth will involve new or existing markets and products.

There are a number of further product and market decisions that are normally required.

Market Categories

First, decisions must be made about the categories of markets that the business will be involved with. The organisation will have to reach decisions on geographic coverage, international exposure and the benefits and risks that attend such options.

Product Features

Second, decisions must be made on the features that the product will possess. The mix of product benefits that a product will possess will not only strongly affect costs, but also the position that the product will assume in the market. We encountered Kotler's (1997) five 'levels' of product features (or 'benefits') and the inclusion or 'leaving out' of any of these will have a strong bearing upon any proposed strategy.

Product and Market Portfolios

Third, product and market decisions must include a consideration of portfolio. The extent to which the products and markets are focused or spread can be very important. A broad portfolio (presence in many product market sectors) offers the advantages of the ability to withstand a downturn in one sector and to exploit opportunities that arise in any of the areas in which the business operates. Conversely, a narrow portfolio enables the organisation's management to be more focused and to develop expertise in its narrower field of operation.

Life Cycle Considerations

The final consideration to be made for products and markets concerns their life cycle positions. It is perhaps intuitively obvious to say that products or markets that are approaching late maturity or are in decline should be of particular concern, but there is also a need to produce new products or develop new markets on an ongoing basis.

Strategic Method Decisions

The third area for which strategic business level decisions are required relates to the methods or mechanisms that are to be used. A basic choice exists between internal (organic) development, mergers and takeovers, and some form of joint development such as alliances and franchising. The choice has important implications for:

- the resources that are required;
- the degree of control over future strategic decisions;
- the speed with which a change in the position of the SBU could be achieved;
- the need to re-configure the internal value chain of the organisation.

For example, organic growth is normally viewed as a slower means of growth (since resources are provided by one organisation only), than either some form of joint development or a merger or takeover, which involve a *step change* in size. However, internal growth retains full control within the existing organisation with no control being ceded to other organisations.

Applying Evaluation Criteria

Identifying the Criteria

When considering which course of action to pursue, it is normally the case that a number of options present themselves to an organisation's top management. In order to ensure that each option is fairly and equally assessed, a number of criteria are applied.

For each option, four criteria are applied – questions to ask of each option. In order to 'pass', the option must usually receive an affirmative answer to each one. In some texts various acronyms are introduced to describe the criteria such as RACES (as described by Haberberg and Rieple, 2001), SCARE and CARES, which usually stand for Resources, Acceptable, Consistent, Effective and Sustainability, which are considered in the order required by the acronym. Here another widely used scheme is used: the SFA framework of Suitability, Feasibility and Acceptability, to which is added a fourth criterion, that of achieving competitive advantage. Thus, each strategic option should be considered in relation to the four criteria by considering whether:

1. the strategic option is *suitable;*
2. the strategic option is *feasible;*
3. the strategic option is *acceptable;*
4. the strategic option will enable the organisation to *achieve competitive advantage.*

The process of evaluation is an integral part of the overall strategy process as indicated in Figure 2.1.

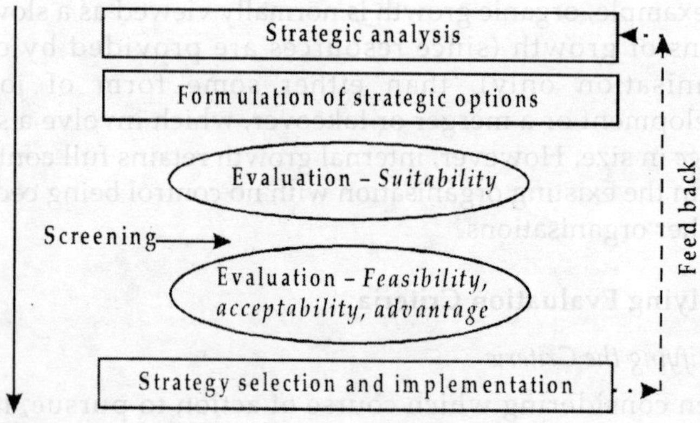

Figure 2.1: The strategic evaluation process.

Suitability Criteria

A strategic option is suitable if it will enable the organisation actually to achieve its strategic objectives. If it will in any way fall short of achieving these objectives, then there is no point in pursuing it and the option should be discarded.

If, for example, an organisation's objective is to spread its market portfolio by gaining a presence in foreign markets, then the option of increasing the company's investment in its domestic home would clearly be unsuitable.

The suitability of options must be assessed not only in relation to the objectives that have been set but also in relation to the SWOT. Options might be regarded as suitable when they:

- exploit *opportunities* in the environment and avoid the *threats;*
- capitalise on an organisation's *strengths* and avoid or address the *weaknesses;*
- address the expectations of key stakeholder groups.

It is also important to recognise cases where strategic options may be unsuitable. For example:

- there may be options that are more suitable so that suitability might be seen in relative terms and the various options ranked according to their suitability;
- there is a need for internal consistency in the choice of options; in that the choice of competitive strategy (such as cost leadership or differentiation) the development direction (such as market development or diversification) and the development method (internal, acquisition or joint development) need to work together as a 'package' (Johnson and Scholes, 2002).

For example, a non-American airline seeking to grow through market penetration of a quality differentiated product in the large US aviation market (which accounts for over 40% of world demand) would be restricted in its choice of strategic method. Foreign ownership restrictions prevent the purchase of American airlines or the development of airlines by foreign based companies, leading to the need to develop joint development opportunities through alliance relationships (such as the longstanding strategic alliance between KLM and Northwest Airlines) to enter this important market.

Table 2.1 presents some examples of why some options might be regarded as sample in terms of specific directions or methods of development.

Screening

Having applied the suitability criterion a further stage might be included in some cases– that of *screening*. If certain options are clearly unsuitable it makes little sense going through the time, effort and expense involved in applying the further criteria. Consequently, at the screening stage a decision is made as to whether it is worth continuing with the further stages of evaluation or that certain options should be disregarded at this stage of evaluation owing to their unsuitability.

Feasibility

A strategic option might be considered to be suitable only to be later found not to be possible. In other words, the option is not feasible. When evaluating options using this criterion, it is likely that the options will be feasible to varying degrees. Some will be completely unfeasible, others 'might be' feasible, whilst others still are definitely so.

Feasibility studies are often carried out prior to tourism projects being approved in order to secure financing.

The extent to which an option is feasible will depend in practice upon the following two areas.

1. Internal Considerations – Culture, Skills and Resources

Culture, skills and resources are internally controlled by the organisation. An organisation might not have the culture, skills or resources which are necessary to carry out the options. A deficit in any of the key resource areas (physical resources, financial, operational human and intellectual) will present a problem at this stage of evaluation. If an option requires capital that is unavailable, human skills that are

Table 2.1: Some Examples of Suitability

Strategic option	*Why this option might be suitable in terms of :*			
Directions	*Environment*	*Resources/competences*	*Expectations*	*Examples*
Consolidation	Withdraw from declining markets Sell valuable assests Maintain market share.	Build on strengths through continued investment and innovation.	Better returns at low risk by exploiting current strategies.	Declining American seaside resort of Atlantic City redeveloped as a gambling destination.
Market penetration	Gain market share for advantage.	Exploit superior resources and competences.		Growth of multiple branch travel agencies in UK during the 1980s and 1990s.
Product development	Exploit knowledge of customer needs.	Exploit expertise in developing new or improved product offerings.	Better returns at medium risk by exploiting current strengths or market knowledge.	Development of all-weahter tourism products such as Center Parcs for Northern Europe.
Market development	Current markets saturated New opportunities for: geographical spread, entering new segments or new uses for existing products.	Exploit current product Portfolio.		Growth of hitherto UK outbound tour operators such as Airtours and Thomson into intenational markets during 1990s, particularly Scandinavia, Germany and North America.

cont.

Strategic option	*Why this option might be suitable in terms of :*			
Directions	*Environment*	*Resources/competences*	*Expectations*	*Examples*
Diversification	Current markets saturated or declining.	Exploit core competences in new arenas.	Better returns at higher risk.	Diversification of Disney Corporation during the 1990s into cruising.
Methods				
Internal development	First in field providing *first mover* advantage Cautious controlled development.	Learning and competence development Spread out the cost.	Cultural and political ease Less disruptive.	Development of low cost 'no frills' airline concept by Southwest Airlines from late 1970s.
Merger/ acquisition	Speed of development Alter supply/ demand balance Improved ratios.	Acquire competences Scale and scope economies.	Returns in terms of growth or enhanced share value Problems of culture clash.	The acquisition of Holland-America and Seabourn cruise lines by Carnival Cruise Lines during the 1990s.
Joint development	Speed Access to markets Industry norm.	Complementary competences Learning from partners	Required for market entry Dilutes risk Fashionable.	The development of franchising by Holiday Inn from the 1950s onwards first in the USA followed by elasewhere in the world.

Source: Adapted from Johnson and Scholes (2002).

difficult to buy in, land or equipment that is equally difficult to obtain or a scarce intellectual resource, then it is likely to fail the feasibility criteria.

For example, London's Heathrow Airport has been working at or close to capacity for a number of years. Take off and landing slots are a scarce resource and are controlled through the rights of airlines which have operated at the airport for a protracted length of time (so-called *grandfather rights*). Many airlines would like to establish a presence at Heathrow as a key international transit hub but are prevented from doing so by the lack of slots. Consequently, whilst establishing a presence at Heathrow might be a *suitable* aspect of a growth strategy it would not be *feasible* owing to the deficit in a key resource area, i.e. the failure to gain access to the physical resource of Heathrow.

The checklist shown as Figure 2.2 indicates some of the key internal feasibility issues to consider.

2. External Considerations – Competitive Reaction

The second area that needs to be considered with regard to feasibility relates to the consideration of competitive reactions and other considerations which are external to the organisation. Specifically, the acceptance of customers and suppliers, competitive reactions and necessary approvals from government or regulatory bodies needs to be considered (Lynch, 2000).

For example, a UK air-inclusive tour operator might wish to double its capacity within one year as part of its growth strategy. Given its past growth record, its financial position and its potential customer base this might appear a suitable strategic option. However, such capacity is licensed in the UK through the Air Tour Organiser's Licence (ATOL) system administered by the Civil Aviation Authority (CAA, a government body). The CAA might take the view that such growth in one year was excessive and financially unsustainable. Consequently, allowable growth might be limited. Hence, what might appear to be suitable strategy is not feasible due to the lack of regulatory approval.

- Capital investment required: do we have the funds?
- Projection of cumulative profits: is it sufficiently profitable?
- Working capital requirements: do we have enough working capital?
- Tax liabilities and dividend payments: what are the implications, especially on timing?
- Number of employees and, in the case of redundancy, any costs associated with this?
- New technical skills required, new operational equipment required: do we have the skills? Do we need to recruit or temporarily hire some specialists?
- New products and how are they to be developed: are we confident that we have a portfolio of fully tested new products? Are they breakthrough products or merely catch-up on our competition?
- Amount and timing of marketing investment and expertise required: do we have the funds? When will they be required? Do we have the specialist expertise such as advertising and promotions agency teams to deliver our strategic options?
- The possibility of acquisition, merger or joint venture with other organisations and the implications: have we fully explored other strategic options that would bring their own benefits and problems?
- Communication of ideas to all those involved: how will this be done? Will we gain the commitment of the managers and employees affected who are required to implement the required changes?

Figure 2.2: Checklist on internal feasibility (adapted from Lynch, 2000).

The checklist shown as Figure 2.3 indicates some of the key internal feasibility issues to consider.

- How will our customers respond to the strategies we are proposing?
- How will our competitors react? Do we have the necessary resources to respond?
- Do we have the necessary support from our suppliers?
- Do we need government or regulatory approval? How likely is this?

Figure 2.3: Checklist on external feasibility (adapted from Lynch, 2000).

Acceptability

Acceptability is concerned with the expected performance outcomes of a strategy. Consequently, the acceptability of a chosen strategy is often determined by using a range of analytical financial and non-financial tools such as those described later in the chapter. A strategic option is acceptable if those who must agree to the strategy accept the option. This raises an obvious question – who are those who agree that the option is acceptable?

The extent that stakeholders can exert influence upon an organisation's strategic decision-making rests upon the two variables, power and interest. Stakeholders that have the highest combination of both the ability to influence (power) and the willingness to influence (interest) will have the most *effective* influence. Where two or more stakeholder groups have comparable influence, the possibility of conflict over acceptability will be heightened. In most cases, the board of directors will be the most influential stakeholder. It is also important to consider the commitment from managers and employees. If important members of the organisation are not committed to the strategy it is unlikely to be successfully implemented.

For example, in the mid-1990s when the previously state owned British Airways was endeavouring to place its strategic emphasis on controlling its hitherto high cost base, it tried to change the working conditions of its cabin staff. Management tried to push through the changes in a way that showed little respect for the views of employees (Haberberg and Rieple, 2001). The dispute resulted in strike action during 1997 and the airline, having underestimated the power of this group of stakeholders, lost many millions of pounds and its reputation for customer service which had been assiduously built up over the preceding few years was seriously eroded.

Competitive Advantage

One of the key objectives in strategy is to create competitive advantage. This criterion asks a simple question of any strategic option – what is the point of pursuing an option if it isn't going to result in superior performance (compared to competitors) or higher than industry-average profitability? In other words, a strategic option would fail this test if it were likely to only result in the business being 'ordinary' or average in relation to the industry or sector norm.

This is particularly important when considering product options. For example, if a new product option is forecast to receive an uncertain reception from the market, we might well ask what is the point of the launch at all. It would be unlikely to result in competitive advantage for the business.

Financial Tools for Evaluation

In the evaluation and selection stage, a number of 'tools' are available to managers which may assist in deciding upon the most appropriate option. Not all of them will be appropriate in every circumstance and some are more widely used than others. They are used to explore the implications of the options so that the decisions that are made are based upon the best possible information.

Accountants or financial analysts are usually very involved in strategic evaluation and selection because of their expertise in understanding the financial implications of the possible courses of action, and the reader is referred to more specialised texts such as Ellis and Williams (1993), Atkinson *et al.* (1995), Kotas and Conlan (1997) and Ambrosini *et al.* (1998), for further coverage. There are two major areas of financial analysis.

Cash Flow Forecasting

One of the most straightforward financial tools is cash flow analysis – sometimes called funds-flow analysis. Many businesses fail not because they fail to be profitable but because have run out of cash, i.e. they become insolvent in that they are unable to pay their bills as they become due. A business may have substantial assets such as cruise ships, aircraft and buildings, but creditors such as suppliers and staff need to be paid in cash.

Essentially, cash flow forecasting involves a forecast of the expected income from an option, of the costs that will be incurred and, from this, the forecast net cash inflows or outflows. For most options, the forecast will be broken down into monthly 'chunks' and a statement will be constructed for each month in which cash outflows and inflows are shown together with opening and closing bank balances. The closing bank balance in one month becomes the opening balance in the following month. The forecast allows for potential problems and solutions to be identified. If the same procedure is carried out for each option, the most favourable can be identified or suggestions can be made in order to improve the forecast cash position. The example from Eurojet below shows a cash flow forecast for a tour operator which experiences seasonal cash flow difficulties.

Cash Flow Forecasting for Eurojet

Eurojet is a fictitious tour operator with ambitious growth plans based upon a clear strategy involving market penetration based upon organic growth and differentiation. This company plans to increase its sales turnover by around 25% each year. However, like many tour operators and travel agents, the company experiences seasonal cash flow difficulties.

A cash flow forecast has been prepared for the following financial year and this is shown below. Figures in the table are in £000s.

	1	*2*	*3*	*4*	*5*	*6*	*7*	*8*	*9*	*10*	*11*	*12*	*Total*
INFLOWS													
Receipts from debtors	230	250	120	50	60	75	80	90	110	150	220	320	1755
Dividend on investment							45						45
TOTAL INFLOWS	230	250	120	50	60	75	125	90	110	150	220	320	1800
OUTFLOWS													
Payments to creditors		80		80		88		88		88		92	516
Wages and other expenses	102	77	58	103	79	59	105	80	62	108	83	63	979
Payments for				70	10	15					5		100

fixed assets													
Dividend payable			80										80
Corporation Tax									120				120
TOTAL OUTFLOWS	102	157	138	253	89	162	105	168	182	196	88	155	1795
NET IN/OUT	128	93	–18	–203	–29	–87	20	–78	–72	–46	132	165	5
Bank balance													
opening	30	158	251	233	30	1	–86	–66	–144	–216	–262	–130	
closing	158	251	233	30	1	–86	–66	–144	–216	–262	–130	35	

a. As a tour operator most funds are received by customers as a deposit and subsequent payment of balance. On average this results in 3 months credit being granted to customers.

b. On average 6 weeks credit is taken from customers.

c. Capital expenditure budget:

New computer facilities	Month 4	£40,000
Routine replacement of motor vehicles	Month 4	£30,000
Computer sofware and programming costs	Month 5	£10,000
Progress payment on building extensions	Month 7	£15,000
Office furniture and equipment	Month 11	£5,000

d. Negotiated overdraft facilities currently stand at £60,000.

Investment Appraisal

An investment, at its simplest, is some money put up for a project in the expectation that it will enable more money to be made in the future. The questions surrounding investment appraisal concern *how much* will be organisation make against each investment option (called the *return* on investment)?

There is a strong time element to investment appraisal techniques because the returns on the investment may remain for several years or even decades. It is for this reason that a factor is often built into the calculation to account for inflation.

Key measures of acceptability are the returns that are likely to accrue from specific options and the risks of potential losses. Returns are based upon forecasts. What risks arise if the forecast returns turn out to be inaccurate? One approach is 'what if?' or sensitivity analysis. Uncertainty is concerned with the risk, that some potential factors affecting returns cannot be forecast but arise unexpectedly.

A common method of assessing the financial acceptability of strategic options is through the application of investment appraisal techniques. Various methods of investment appraisal can be used which are briefly considered below.

Payback Method

The first and most obvious thing that accountants want to know about any investment is the *payback period.* This is the time taken to repay the investment – the shorter the better. If, the example, an investment of £1000 is expected to increase profits by £100 a month, then the payback period will be 10 months.

In practice, payback periods are rarely this short and it is this fact that makes investment appraisal calculations a bit more complicated. When the effects of inflation are taken into account, the returns on an investment can be eroded over time. Consequently, accountants include a factor to account for the effects of inflation, usually on a 'best-guess' basis. The payback method can be justified on the grounds that it represents a simple, quick screening process. However, it can be criticised in that it ignores the so-called 'time value of money' and also ignores inflows after the payback period.

Accounting Rate of Return (ARR)

The ARR is, as its title implies, an accounting measure. It is calculated in three steps:

1. Take average annual inflows over project life.
2. Deduct depreciation on the initial outlay.
3. Divide result by the average investment over the period.

The ARR can be justified (like the payback method) on the grounds that it represents a simple, quick screening process but can be criticised in that it ignores the so-called 'time value of money'.

Discounted Cash Flow (DCF) Methods

DCF methods (Net present value and internal rate of return) are considered superior (but more complicated) than payback and ARR because such methods consider the timing of cash flows – *the time value of money.* The time value of money is based on the notion that companies or individuals need to be compensated for foregoing the use of money for a period of time if it has been invested in a project. Such methods are based on the concept of compound interest in reverse. If, for example, interest rates are 10% and a certain investment promises to pay $100,000 in 1 year's time, the amount we would need to invest now is:

$$\frac{\$100{,}000 \times 100}{110} = \$90{,}909$$

i.e. $90,909 now is equivalent to $100,000 received in 1 year. It is the *present value* of $100,000.

Net Present Value (NPV)

NPV is the value obtained by discounting the forecast cash inflows and outflows of a project at a chosen *acceptable* rate of return and taking the net total. If NPV is positive then the investment is worthwhile; if it is negative, the project or option should be rejected.

Internal Rate of Return (IRR)

The goal with this method is to find the interest rate at which inflow exactly equal outflows, i.e. where NPV = 0. Where IRR is higher than the rate deemed to be an acceptable level of return then the option should be considered as financially viable. For example, if 10% is viewed as an acceptable rate of return and IRR is calculated to be 15% then the project would be deemed to be viable.

NPV and IRR Compared

IRR is easier to understand (because it is expressed as a percentage) but NPV is normally considered superior because:

1. NPV is easier to calculate.
2. IRR ignores relative size of the investment.
3. IRR rates are non-additive, i.e. the rates from two or more projects cannot be added together.
4. In some circumstances there may be more than one IRR.

A full consideration of investment appraisal techniques is beyond the scope of this chapter. A number of books, such as Dyson (2001), consider the topic in greater depth.

Limitations of the Financial Tools

The limitations of the financial tools rest in the problem of the unpredictability of the future. The macro- and micro-environments can change – sometimes rapidly. Accordingly, the actual returns that an organisation makes on an investment may not always be what were expected.

A similar limitation applies to forecasting the level of inflation for net present value calculations. In the major First World economies such as those in Western Europe, North America, Japan and Australia, the level of inflation has historically been relatively stable at between 2 and 10%, with an occasional 'shock' such as in the mid-1970s when, in the UK, it reached 24% because of a quadrupling of oil prices caused by a Middle-Eastern conflict. In other parts of the world, however, problems with the supply of goods and the value of currency can lead to much higher inflation levels – sometimes exceeding 1000% a year. A presumption of low and stable inflation will therefore tend to encourage investment rather than high and unpredictable inflation.

Other Tools for Evaluation

Financial evaluation of strategic options is very important, but for most organisations, other tools can also provide useful information. These may require financial information as an input and so they should be seen not as 'instead of' financial analyses, but 'as well as'. They enrich the information enabling management to select the best strategic option.

Cost-benefit Analysis

Cost-benefit analysis applies to almost every area of life, not just strategic evaluation and selection. The cost-benefit concept suggests that a money value can be put on all costs and benefits of a strategy, including tangible and intangible returns to people and organisations proposing the project. Each option will have a cost associated with it and will be expected to return certain benefits. If both of these can be quantified in financial terms, then the cost-benefit calculation will be relatively straightforward. The problem is that this is rarely the case.

The costs of pursuing one particular option will have a number of elements. Any financial investment costs will be easily quantifiable. Against this, the cost of not pursuing the next best option needs to be taken into account – the *opportunity cost*. There may also be a number of social and environmental costs which are much harder to attach a value to.

The same problems apply to the benefits. In addition to financial benefits, an organisation may also take into account social benefits and others such as improved reputation or improved service. Intangible benefits are very difficult to attach a value to for a cost-benefit analysis as they can take a long time to work through to increased financial performance.

Whilst it is difficult to quantify non-financial benefits it is usually possible after some calculations have been made and often negotiations and research amongst the interested parties. Certainly the technique is commonly used to assess the acceptability of strategic options, particularly in the public sector (Williams and Giardina, 1993) and in cases where development involves public-private partnerships. The problem in many cases is to know just where the analysis should stop.

For example, in considering a major new airport development for a city it would seem appropriate that the increased costs of noise and emission pollution and congestion for the city should be costed. However, aircraft emissions are thought to be partly responsible for the global warming phenomena. Consequently, should the costs associated with global warming arising from increased air transport movements also be factored into the calculations or is this aspect too remote from the project under consideration?

KEY CONCEPT: SOCIAL COSTS AND BENEFITS

All organisations have an impact upon the societies that are in their locality or that are affected by their products or activities. Although the term *social* is a bit nebulous, it is generally taken to mean the effect on the condition of employment, social well-being, health, chemical emissions, pollution, aesthetic appearance (e.g. 'eyesores'), charitable societies, etc.

A strategic option will have an element of social cost and social benefit. We would describe a social cost as a deterioration in any of the above – an increase in unemployment, higher levels of emissions, pollution, declining salaries, etc. Conversely, a social benefit will result in an improvement in the condition of society – increasing employment, cleaner industry, better working conditions, etc.

Impact Analysis

When a strategic option may be reasonably expected to have far reaching consequences in either social or financial terms, an impact study may be appropriate. Essentially, this involves asking the question, 'If this option goes ahead, what will its impact be upon the local (regional) environment, community and economy?'

The aspects that might be impacted upon will depend upon the particular circumstances of the option. The impacts have been widely discussed in a travel and tourism context by authors such as Mathieson and Wall (1982), Archer (1996), Wager (1997), Mules (2000) and the World Tourism Organisation (1994).

For a proposed development of a new theme park, for example, the impact study might typically take into account the development's implications for:

- local employment;
- primary and secondary levels of spending to be generated and *leakages* from the local economy;
- the effect of the development on other businesses;
- the capacity of the local infrastructure such as road and rail services but also utilities such as water and sewerage, waste disposal, gas and electricity;
- the environmental impact on the local flora and fauna and the effects of noise pollution;
- the aesthetic impact of the development on the local community.

In many cases, an impact study will be an intrinsic part of the cost-benefit calculation, and it suffers from the same limitations – that of evaluating the true value of each aspect that may be impacted.

'What if?' and Sensitivity Analysis

The uncertainties of the future, as we have seen, make any prediction inexact. Whilst an organisation can never be certain of any sequence of future events, 'what if?' analysis (or scenario planning as it is sometimes called), and its variant, sensitivity analysis, can give an idea of how the outcome would be affected by a number of possible disruptions.

The development of computerised applications such as spreadsheets has made this activity easier than it used to be. A financial model on a spreadsheet that makes a number of assumptions such as revenue projections, cost forecasts, inflation rate, etc., can be modified to instantly show the effect of, say, a 10% increase in costs or a higher-than-expected rate of inflation. This is designed to show how sensitive the cash flow is to its assumptions – hence the name.

For example, an airline might produce a projection of future earnings based on the assumption that the average price it would have to pay for its jet-fuel requirements (a major constituent of airline costs) is US$ 0.60 per gallon. The airline obviously is unable to control the price of this key input and indeed has no accurate means of forecasting it.

Consequently, when forecasting its future earnings the airline might regard it as a prudent step to produce alternative scenarios which ask the 'what if' question. The scenarios might suppose that:

- A major war breaks out or the Organisation of Petroleum Exporting Countries (OPEC) restricts supplies, thereby increasing jet fuel prices by 25%.
- Surplus supplies of jet fuel become available as a result of lower demand for air services leading to jet fuel prices falling by 10%.

Having produced the scenarios and calculated the impact of the events on the cost of jet fuel the airline would factor the costs into its overall calculations. As a result the airline might be able to produce a central or base earnings forecast based on the US$ 0.60 per gallon price, but would also have knowledge of the effect an increase or decrease in fuel costs would have on overall profitability. In other words, the *sensitivity* of earnings to fuel price changes would have been assessed. In some cases the analysis might go a stage further by applying weightings to the scenarios. Thus, the airline might be fairly confident about its central assumption and assign a 50% weighting, i.e. its assessment of the situation is that there is a 50% chance of the central assumption of US$ 0.60 per gallon being realised. Similarly, the company might assess the situation and feel that if the central case is not borne out then a rise is more likely than a fall and consequently 30% and 20% weightings are assigned to the rising and falling fuel price scenarios respectively.

Qualitative variables can also be analysed. If an option has a high dependency upon the availability of a key raw material or the oversight of a key manager, a 'what if?' study will show the effect that the loss or reduction in the key input would have.

Strategic Evaluation in Emergent Strategies

Business strategies can be either deliberate (or prescriptive) or emergent. This is to say that some strategies are planned in advance, often following a rational sequence of events – deliberate strategies. Others are not planned in this way and are said to be emergent – they result from an organisation's management following a consistent pattern of behaviour.

This distinction is important when it comes to strategic evaluation. Companies that employ the deliberate model are likely to use the criteria and the tools above whilst those that prefer the emergent model are less likely to do so explicitly. This is not to say, however, that the analytical process cannot form a part of an intelligent manager's intuitive thinking.

It is here that one of the potential limitations of emergent strategy becomes apparent. If an organisation follows a deliberate process with its systematic and sequential events, then it can be more certain that all possible options have been identified and evaluated before the most appropriate one is selected. An intuitive emergent approach that relies upon patterns of behaviour cannot be certain that the best option is taken in all times of decision. It might get it right – but it might not.

3

STRATEGIC IMPLEMENTATION FOR TRAVEL AND TOURISM ORGANISATIONS

Introduction

Strategic implementation is concerned with the issues which are considered to be necessary for the successful execution of strategy. In a deliberate strategic process, strategic implementation would be carried out only after an organisation has gathered sufficient information on its internal and external environments (this being the purpose of strategic analysis) and after it has undertaken the process of choosing strategic options. The evaluation of these options is followed by the selection of the most appropriate option.

In order to carry out a strategy successfully, an organisation must consider several key areas. First, it must establish how the strategy will be resourced. Second, it should ask itself how well its current culture, structure and internal systems are able to meet the challenges of the strategy. Changes in any or all of these may become necessary. Finally, most strategies necessitate some degree of internal change and this process of change will need to be managed. This chapter discusses each of these matters in turn.

Learning Objectives

After studying this chapter, students should be able to:

- describe where implementation fits into the strategic process;
- describe the role of resource planning in strategic implementation;
- explain how and why corporate culture plays an important part in implementation;
- understand the link between structure and strategy;
- describe the essentials of change management.

Implementation and the Strategic Process

Most people intuitively understand that a lot of information is required before any big decision is made. We wouldn't normally buy a holiday (a relatively expensive purchase) without investigating the attractions of the destination or finding out something about the company we would be travelling with and the accommodation available. In the same way, an organisation or business would be risking a great deal if it were to pursue a strategic option without first carrying out a detailed analysis of its internal and external environments.

Put simply, successful strategy selection and implementation relies upon the presupposition that the organisation has carried out a meaningful strategic analysis and is consequently aware of its internal strengths and weaknesses and its external opportunities and threats. Without being 'armed' with this information, the company cannot be certain that the chosen strategy would be the correct choice. The process leading to implementation is shown in Figure 3.1.

In order to carry out (implement) a strategy successfully, an organisation will need to work out how to resource it. This means how it will obtain the requisite finance, human resources (usually in the form of appropriately skilled employees) and the physical resources such as equipment and buildings. As part of this process a detailed strategy may be developed for each part of the organisation, such as the marketing, finance operations and personnel functional areas. It should also reconfigure its culture and structure to 'fit' the

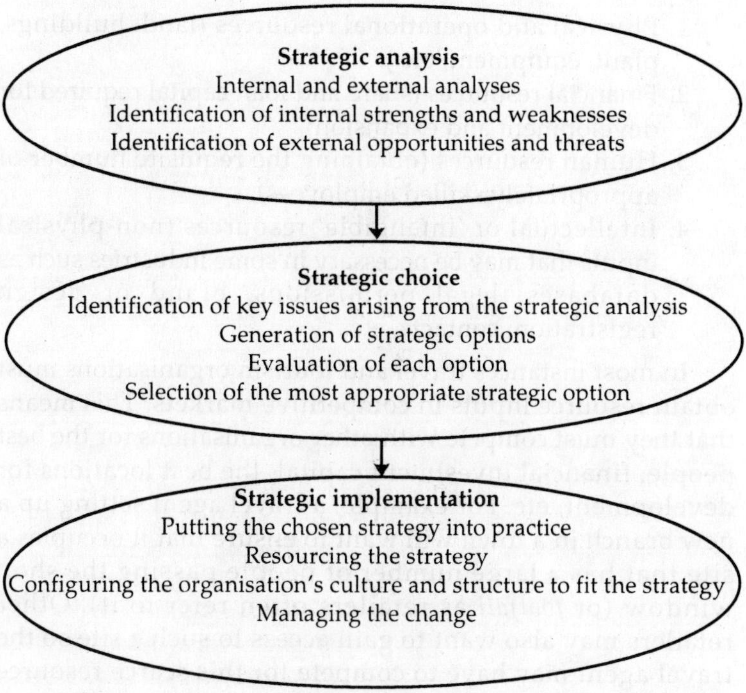

Figure 3.1: The linear-rational (prescriptive) strategic process.

proposed strategy. Finally, strategic implementation often means change inside the organisation in order to achieve the agreed objectives. Change management is thus the third area to be considered in strategic implementation. This chapter will briefly consider each of these issues.

Resources and Implementation

Resources – The Key Inputs

In the same way that people and animals need the inputs of air, food, warmth, etc., so also organisations need inputs in order to function normally. Economics textbooks would refer to these inputs as the *factors of production*. They fall into four broad categories:

1. Physical and operational resources (land, buildings, plant, equipment, etc.).
2. Financial resources (share and loan capital required for development and expansion).
3. Human resources (obtaining the requisite number of appropriately skilled employees).
4. Intellectual or 'intangible' resources (non-physical inputs that may be necessary in some industries such as databases, legal permissions, brand or design registration, contacts, etc.

In most instances travel and tourism organisations must obtain resource inputs in competitive markets. This means that they must compete with other organisations for the best people, financial investment capital, the best locations for development, etc. For example, a travel agent setting up a new branch in a town will want to ensure that it occupies a site that has a large number of people passing the shop window (or *footfall* as retailers often refer to it). Other retailers may also want to gain access to such a site so the travel agent may have to compete for this scarce resource thus bidding up the price. At some point the price (in the form of rent) may become too great in relation to the expected revenues, so decisions have to made as to how much can be afforded.

Thus all of these inputs have a cost attached to them and so careful planning for resource requirement is usually a key calculation in strategic implementation.

Matching Strategy with Resources

Once a strategic option has been settled upon (following the strategic choice stage), management attention turns to evaluating the resource implications of the strategy. The extent to which the resource base needs to be adjusted will, of course, depend upon the degree of change that the proposed strategy entails.

Broadly speaking, resource planning falls into three categories (Johnson and Scholes, 1998).

Few Changes Strategies

Some strategies, particularly those that are not particularly ambitious, require few changes in the resource base. They may require, for example, a slight increase in financing to fund modest expansion or the recruitment or retraining of some human resources to meet a skill shortage in one or two areas. Conversely, of course, a few changes strategy may require the disposal of some assets or a slight reduction in the human resource base.

Resource Increase Strategies

Second, some strategies require an increase in the resource base in order to facilitate a more substantial programme of growth. This usually entails two things: an internal reallocation of resources and the purchasing of fresh resource inputs from external resource suppliers. Internal reallocation entails reducing resource employment in one area of the organisation and moving it across to where it is needed, say by redeploying human resources or by selling some non-core activities to reinvest the money in the area of growth. New resources (from outside the organisation) are obtained through the usual channels – from the job-market, the real estate market, the financial markets and so on.

Resource Decrease Strategies

Third, some strategies involve a reduction in the resource base in order to manage decline successfully. If an organisation finds, after a resource audit, that it has too many resources (say too many employees, too many aircraft, too many hotel properties in the wrong locations, etc.) then measures are put in place to carry out some reduction. Excess capital or physical resources can often be successfully reinvested in business areas that are in more buoyant markets whilst excess human resources must usually be released.

KEY CONCEPT: RESOURCE AUDIT

An audit process can be used to make assessments of any or all of the resource inputs. In some depth the human resource audit, but the same procedures can be employed to audit financial, physical or intellectual resources.

The nature or audit of any kind (including resource audits) is of purposeful checking or testing. Resources are audited (or purposefully checked) for:

- *sufficiency* (is there enough for the purpose?)
- *adequacy* (is the condition, location, state, or quality of the resource adequate for the purpose?)
- *availability* (are the required resources available at the time and in the quantities required?)

An audit of a hotel group's chain of hotels (an example of physical resources) might take the form of assessing whether the number of rooms is *sufficient* for current needs and any planned expansion. This might be followed by an evaluation of *adequacy* – the location of the hotels relative to customers and those of competitors; the state of repair and decoration of the hotels; and, the ability of the hotels to support the prevailing business (leisure, business, conferences, etc.). Finally, if more resources are required or if development of the land or buildings is needed, *availability* is examined, either of additional property or of permissions for development.

Developing and Controlling Resources

In order to meet the resource requirements of a proposed strategy, resources are developed and then controlled to ensure they meet the needs of the strategy.

Financial Resource Planning

Financial resource planning takes the form of financing the proposed strategy. *Capital budgeting* concerns projecting the capital needs of a strategy. This is usually a relatively straightforward operation as costs can normally be forecast with some accuracy. Once the capital requirements are known, a plan is put in place to finance any shortfall. Whilst some strategies can be financed from retained profits (depending upon how much retained profit the company has), others are financed from external sources such as share (rights) issues, debt capital or the issuing of corporate bonds or debentures.

Human Resource Planning

Human resource planning involves projecting the human capital required for the successful implementation of the proposed strategy. It would typically take the form of forecasts of both the numbers of people required and the types of skills and abilities that will be in demand. If a shortfall in either of these is identified, the 'gap' will be filled by one or more of the following.

- Training, retraining or staff development – to close the skills gap by developing existing employees.
- Appointing new employees – entering the labour market and competing with other employers for the requisite number of appropriately skilled employees.

Physical and Operational Resource Planning

Physical resource planning is slightly more complex than financial and human resource planning. The reason for this is that so many inputs fall into this category. We include in this category land, buildings, location, plant and equipment.

Some physical resources are more easily obtained than others. Most equipment is relatively easily obtained, unless the requirement is very specialised. However, careful planning may be necessary for some equipment needs require long lead times for their construction. For example, a cruise line or an airline seeking to update its fleet with new ships or aircraft would need to plan one or two years in advance in order to secure delivery on a particular date. Businesses that have requirements for key locations and buildings of particular specificity expose themselves to the possibility of having to settle for second best if they are unable effectively to compete in these particular resource markets.

Some sectors of the travel and tourism industry exemplify this competition for physical resources. The location of a travel retail outlet, a hotel or a visitor attraction will often be a key determinant in the success of the business. Successfully competing with competitors for prime locations and the best buildings will consequently be of paramount importance, especially when these locations are in short supply. Hong Kong has developed in Hong Kong island (where the Central Business District CBD is located) and across the harbour in Kowloon on the Chinese mainland. On the island, especially in Central' (the CBD), the lack of suitable sites and the costs of development have forced hotels to seek other locations. Banks and other financial institutions have been willing to pay very high prices for prime sites, and consequently many of the new hotel developments have taken place elsewhere on the island or in Kowloon, where development sites are more plentiful and where land costs are lower. The Hilton Hotel in Central, for example, was demolished to make way for an office development.

Intellectual Resource Planning

Intellectual resources – inputs that cannot be seen and touched – can be the most important resource inputs of all. Some proposed strategies have a requirement for a legal or regulatory permission, a database (say of key customers in a certain market segment), or experience of dealing with certain markets.

Organisational Culture and Implementation

Culture Suitability

Strategic implementation usually involves making an assessment of the suitability of a culture to undertake the strategy. In the same way that human personalities differ in their readiness to undertake certain courses of action, so also some organisational 'personalities' differ.

In the context of implementation, culture is usually analysed for its suitability. If we consider human personalities, we can readily appreciate that not all personalities are equally suitable for all jobs or tasks.

Some people, for example, have a personality that is ready to embrace a new challenge and who take to change with vigour and excitement. They enjoy bungee jumping and parachute jumps. Other people prefer things not to change.

They are conservative in nature and they would be likely to turn down the opportunity to engage in risky sports. These two personality types highlight the suitability contrasts that can exist.

Handy (1993) identified four types of culture – power, role, task and person. Miles and Snow (1978) also identified four culture types by their reaction tendency, and this is probably the more useful typology in this context.

Miles and Snow's Typology and Cultural Postures

Miles and Snow's (1978) typology divided culture types according to how they approach strategy. These distinctions are important as they tell us how each culture type will react to different strategic options.

A Review of the Miles and Snow Categories

Defender cultures are suitable for organisations that exist in relatively well-defined market areas and where improving the position in existing markets is the most appropriate strategic option (e.g. market penetration). The culture would feel uncomfortable with having to develop new markets or diversification. The values resident within defender cultures work well if markets are stable and relatively mature.

Prospector cultures, in contrast to defenders, are continually seeking out new product and market opportunities. Accordingly, they often create change and uncertaintly. The cultural norms within the culture are consequently more able to develop new markets and products.

Analyser cultures exhibit features of both defenders and prospectors. They have developed a culture that is able to accommodate both stability (which defenders like) and instability (which prospectors have learned to adjust to). The culture can be formal in some circumstances and flexible and 'organic' in others.

Reactor cultures can sometimes lack strategic focus and are consequently sometimes accused of being 'blown around' by changes in their environments. They do not innovate and tend to emulate the successes of competitors.

The Purpose of Examining Miles and Snow's Typology

It is evident that the ability of cultures to undertake different strategic courses of action varies. It is likely, for example, that defender cultures and those like them would be less able to undertake a programme of radical change than, say, those that exhibit prospector characteristics.

Cultural differences between *what is* and *what is required* for a strategy is one of the most important aspect of strategic implementation. Incongruities between the two present a challenge to management in respect of either changing the culture or compromising on strategic objectives such that cultural change is required to a lesser extent. We will return to the nature of change including cultural change – later in this chapter.

Cultural Change at British Airways

During the 1970s and 1980s the publicly owned British airline British Airways or 'BA', as it was commonly referred to, had become synonymous with poor service. The common joke of the time was that BA stood for 'bloody awful'. Despite recent indifferent performance British Airways is often put forward as a successful example of cultural change. After the airline went public by floating on the stock exchange in 1987 a major cultural change programme was introduced which emphasised the service-led orientation of the business. Virtually the entire 37,000 workforce was put through a two-day culture-change training course entitled 'Putting People First'. Almost all of the airline's 1,400 managers went through a five-day version entitled 'Managing People First'. What separated this programme from most normal management training programmes was its size, the consistency with which it was applied throughout the organisation to all grades of employees, and the determination of senior management to drive the programme through.

The programme's emphasis was on instilling a new culture, but this ran alongside other changes. An appraisal scheme was introduced which measured not only what managers did but how they went about it and bonuses were introduced. An emphasis was also placed on informing staff of the competitive pressures facing the airline and on empowering staff to make decisions on their own initiative rather than being bound by inflexible rules.

Source: Adapted from Tushman and O'Reilly (1996).

Structure and Implementation

What is Structure?

Organisational structure refers to the 'shape' of the business. The importance of structure to strategic success is intuitively easy to grasp by using the structure of a human body as a metaphor. Some people are naturally large and may be slightly overweight whilst others are smaller, lithe and fit. The skeletal and muscle structure of people is a major determinant of their suitability for certain activities. People who are large and overweight are less suitable for ballet dancing but are more suitable as sumo wrestlers or as members of tug-of-war teams. Conversely, smaller and fitter people are better at running, rowing and competitive horseracing.

There is no such thing as 'the perfect structure' since usually compromises have to be made in their design and often they are the result of ad hoc growth where parts are added over time rather than planned from the outset. However, in relation to strategy it is necessary to consider whether the proposed structure is capable of helping the organisation achieve the objectives that have been set as part of its strategy. Organisational structures tend to be described in terms of their 'height', their 'width' and their 'complexity'. A fourth, related way of describing organisational structures is according to their method of division.

The 'Height' of Structures

Height refers to the number of layers that exist within the structure. It is perhaps intuitively obvious that larger organisations are higher than smaller ones. The guide to how high an organisational structure should be depends upon the complexity of the tasks that a proposed strategy entails. A small, single site travel agent is involved in competing in one location with an easily identified number of competitors and a single set of product types. This scenario is much less complex than a multinational, vertically and horizontally integrated travel company that competes in many national markets, in several product types and with a high dependence on innovation.

Essentially, height facilitates the engagement of specialist managers in the middle of an organisation who can oversee and direct the many activities that some large organisations are involved in. Not all organisations have this requirement and it would be more appropriate for such organisations to have a flatter structure (see Figure 3.2). The trend in recent years has been for organisations to become flatter as increasingly technology can provide information directly from the point of sale to the highest levels. This process is often known as *delayering* and facilitates quicker decision-making and the faster communications between managers and operational employees who have to implement the decisions.

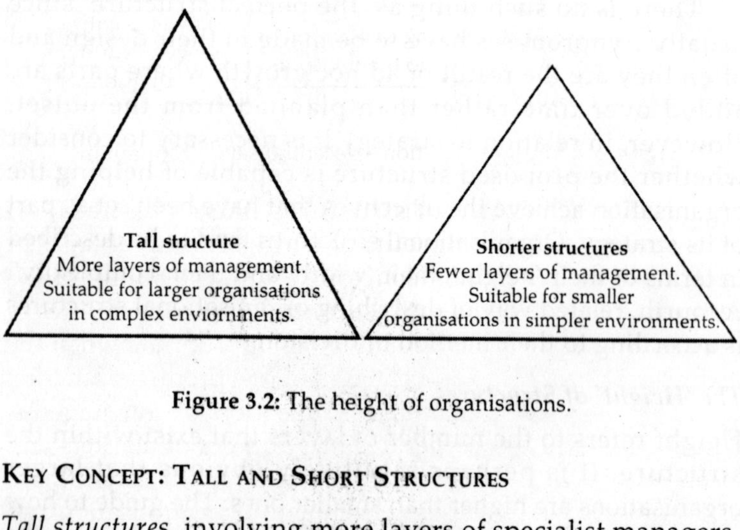

Figure 3.2: The height of organisations.

Key Concept: Tall and Short Structures

Tall structures, involving more layers of specialist managers, enable the organisation to coordinate a wider range of activities across different product and market sectors. It is more difficult for senior management to control and is obviously more expensive in terms of management overhead.

Shorter structures involve few management layers and are suitable for smaller organisations that are engaged in few products or market structures. They are cheaper to operate and facilitate a greater degree of senior management control.

The 'Width' of Structures

The 'width' of organisational structures refers to the extent to the organisation is centralised or decentralised. A decentralised organisational structure is one in which the centre elects to devolve some degree of decision-making power to other parts of the organisation. A centralised organisation is one in which little or no power is devolved from the centre. In practice, a continuum exists between the two extremes along which the varying extents of decentralisation can be visualised (see Figure 3.3).

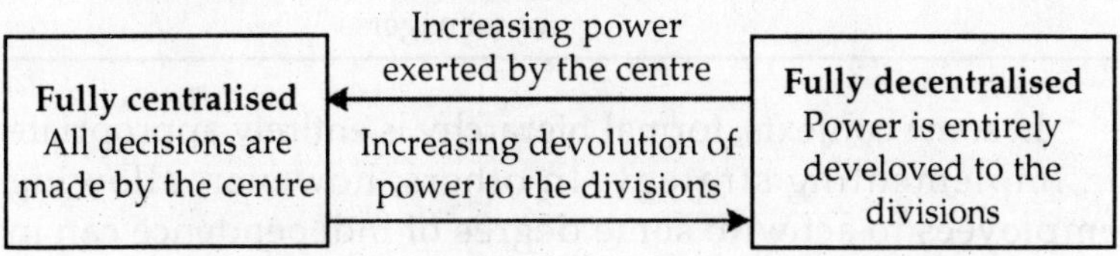

Figure 3.3: The centralisation – decentralisation continuum.

As with the height of structures, there is a trade-off between the costs and benefits of width. The advantages of centralisation are mainly concerned with the ability of the centre to maintain tighter direct control over the activities of the organisation. This is usually more appropriate when the organisation is smaller and engages in few product or market segments. Some degree of decentralisation is advantageous when the organisation operates in a number of markets and localised specialised knowledge is an important determinant of overall success. The main advantages of centralisation and centralisation are summarised in Table 3.1

Complexity of Structure

The complexity of structure is usually taken to mean the extent to which the organisation observes formal hierarchy in its reporting relationships. Strict hierarchy is not always an appropriate form of organisation, especially when it cannot be automatically assumed that seniority guarantees superior management skill.

Table 3.1
The Advantages of Centralisation and Decentralisation (which have both Horizontal and Vertical Lines of Reporting)

Advantages of centralisation	*Advantages of decentralisation*
Managers at centre maintain tight control.	Can engage in a wider range of activities.
Avoids problems of complex structures.	Enables increased specialisation.
Communications quicker and cheaper.	Can reduce time taken to make key decisions.
Delegation risks avoided.	Can develop and improve the skills of managers.

In some contexts, formal hierarchy is entirely appropriate in implementing strategy. In others, however, allowing employees to act with some degree of independence can in fact enable the organisation to be more efficient. The use of so-called matrix structures (which have both horizontal and vertical lines of reporting) for example, can result in the organisation being able to carry out many more tasks than a formal hierarchical structure. Many companies go 'half way' in this regard by seconding employees into special task forces or cross-functional teams that are not part of the hierarchical structure, and which act semi-independently in pursuit of its brief.

Culture and Structure at EasyJet

EasyJet favours an informal company culture with a very flat management structure, which, the company argues, eliminates unnecessary and wasteful layers of management. All office-based employees are encouraged to dress casually. Ties are banned, except for pilots! Remote working (away from the office) and 'hot desking' (sharing desks) have been characteristics of easyJet since the beginning.

Methods of Divisionalisation

The fourth and final way of understanding how structure fits into strategic implementation is by considering how the parts of the organisation are to be divided. As with all of the other matters to be considered in structure, the method of division is entirely dependent upon the context of the company and its strategic position. It is a case of establishing the most appropriate divisional structure to meet the objectives of the proposed strategy.

Divisions are based upon the grouping together of people with a shared specialism. By acting together within their specialism, it is argued that synergies can be obtained both with and between divisions. There are four common methods of divisionalisation:

1. by functional specialism (typically operations, HRM, marketing, finance and operations);
2. by geographic concentration (where divisions are regionally located and have specialised knowledge of local market conditions);
3. by product specialism (where divisions, usually within multi-product companies, have detailed knowledge of their particular products area);
4. by customer focus (where the company orientates itself by divisions dedicated to serving particular customer types, for example retail customers, industrial customers. etc.).

In many cases, a 'hybrid' approach to divisionalisation might be appropriate. For example, a vertically integrated tour operator, airline and travel retailer with sales in the UK, Western Europe and North America might have a hybrid divisional structure with geographical, product, and functional elements as shown in Figure 3.4. Each geographical region might have three product areas (the UK is used in Figure 3.4 for illustration), each having its own functional divisions.

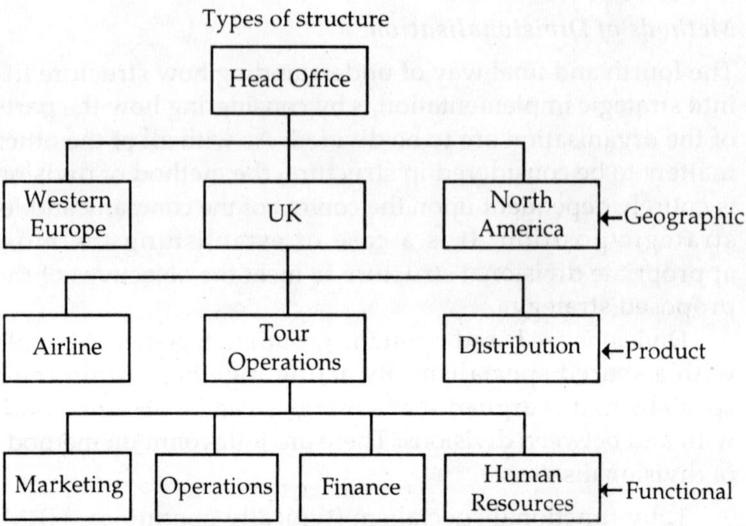

Figure 3.4: An example of a 'hybrid' divisional structure for a vertically integrated travel company.

Managing the Changes in Implementation

The Need for Change

At its simplest, strategy is all about change. In this chapter, we have encountered the importance of an organisation's resource base, its culture and its structure. In order to bring about strategic repositioning (say in respect to products and markets), all of these may need to be changed.

Different organisations exhibit differing attitudes to change. We can draw a parallel here with different types of people. Some people are very conservative and configure their lives so as to minimise change. Such people will generally fear change and will resist it. Other people seem to get bored easily and are always looking for new challenges, new jobs, and so on. Organisations reflect this spectrum of attitudes. It is here that we encounter the concept of *inertia*.

Inertia – Identifying Barriers to Change

Intertia is a term borrowed from physics. It refers to the force that needs to be exerted on a body to overcome its state in relation to its motion. If a body is stationary (i.e. at rest) then we would need to exert a force upon it to make it move. The size and shape of the body will have a large bearing upon its inertia – compare the inertia of a football to that of a train.

In the same way, different organisations present management with varying degrees of inertia. Some are easy to change and others are much more reluctant. The willingness to change may depend upon the culture of the organisation – its size, its existing structure, its product and/or market positioning and even its age (i.e. how long it has existed in its present form).

For most purposes, we can say that resistance to change on the part of employees can be caused by one or more of the following attitudes:

- it may be that those affected by the change *lack an understanding* of the details. They may not have had the reasons for the change explained to them or they may not be aware of how they will personally be affected. This particular barrier can normally be overcome relatively easily by management taking the requisite measures to close the information gap;
- there may be a *lack of trust* on the part of employees in respect to management;
- employee inertia may be based upon fear – particularly in respect to their personal position or their social relationships. Those affected by the change may fear that the proposed changes will adversely affect their place in the structure or the relationships they enjoy in the organisation;
- some inertia is driven by *uncertainty* about the future. Attitudes to uncertainty vary significantly between people, with some showing a much more adverse reaction to it than others.

Kurt Lewin's Three-step Model of Understanding Change

Lewin (1947) suggested that organisational change could be understood in terms of three consecutive processes: unfreezing, moving and then refreezing.

Unfreezing

Unfreezing involves introducing measures that will enable employees to abandon their current practices or cultural norms in preparation for the change. In many organisations nothing has changed for many years and unfreezing is necessary as a 'shaking-up' phase. The impetus for unfreezing can come from either inside or outside the organisation itself. Changing market conditions, for example, sometimes give employees warning that change will be imminent. A particular market crisis may precipitate the expectation amongst employees that change must happen as a result. Internally, a management shake-up, a profit warning or talk of restructuring may bring about similar expectations.

Moving to the New Level

Moving to the new level involves bringing about the requisite change itself. The time period given over to this phase varies widely. Structural change can usually be brought about relatively quickly. Changes in internal systems sometimes take longer (such as the introduction of new quality or information systems), whilst changing culture can take years.

Refreezing

Refreezing is necessary to 'lock in' the changes and to prevent the organisation from going back to its old ways. Again, we would usually take cultural changes to require more 'cementing in' than some other changes and some resolve might be required on the part of senior management.

Step and Incremental Change

The pace at which change happens can usually be divided into one of two categories – step and incremental (see Figure 3.5). There are two factors that determine which is the most appropriate (Quinn and Voyer, 1998).

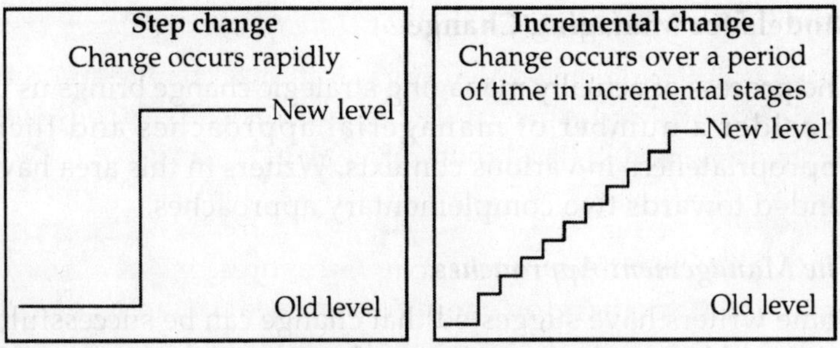

Figure 3.5: Step and incremental change.

1. How urgent the need for change is. A market crisis will typically bring about an urgent need for rapid change whereas preparing for the introduction of a new legal regulation in five years' time will usually allow change to be brought about more slowly and perhaps more painlessly.
2. How much inertia is resident within the organisation's culture. The time taken to unfreeze the inertia in some organisations will necessarily take longer than in others.

Step change offers the advantage of 'getting it over with'. It enables the organisation to respond quickly to changes in its environment and hence enable it to conform to new conditions without lagging behind. Its disadvantages include the 'pain' factor – it may require some coercion or force on the part of management, which in turn may damage employee–management relationships.

Incremental changes offer the advantage of a step-by-step approach to change. For organisations with high inertia, it enables management to gain acceptance before and during the change process, and consequently, it tends to be more inclusive. The process is divided into a number of distinct phases and there may be periods of 'rest' between the phases. It would be an inappropriate technique to use in situations of rapid environmental change.

Models for Managing Change

The process of actually managing strategic change brings us to consider a number of managerial approaches and their appropriateness in various contexts. Writers in this area have tended towards two complementary approaches.

The Management Approaches

Some writers have suggested that change can be successfully managed by employing a range of managerial practices. We can conceive of this approach as an 'if this doesn't work, try this' mechanism.

Most academics and managers have agreed that the process should begin with *education and communication.* The purpose if this is to inform those (usually internal) stakeholders who will be affected by the change. The message communicated will usually contain an explanation of the seasons for the change and an overview of its timescale and extent. In some organisational contexts, this procedure alone will be sufficient to overcome inertia and get the change process under way. In others, this will not be enough.

The next step will thus be to progress to *negotiation* and *participation.* Affected stakeholders will be invited to contribute to the process and to participate in its execution. It is thus hoped, by this process, that employees will be 'on board' – that they will feel some sense of ownership of the change. Some managers may introduce some degree of manipulation (of employees) in this stage, possibly by appealing to the emotional responses of employees or by over- or under-stating the reality of the changes in the environment.

Finally, if all else has failed to bring about the willing participation of the employees, management may be able to introduce some degree of *coercion.* This tactic is far from being appropriate in all contexts, but where it is possible, it can be used to significant effect. Coercion is the practice of forcing through change by exploiting the power asymmetry between executive management and 'rank and file' employees. It is usually only used as a last resort – it can have a very negative effect on management–employee relationships after the change.

The Change Agent Approach

Some texts refer to this approach as the 'champion of change' model. It is a change process that is managed from start to finish by a single individual (or a small team). The individual (or change agent) may be key manager within the organisation or he or she may be brought in as a consultant for the duration of the process.

The change agent approach offers a number of advantages.

First, it provides a focus for the change in the form of a tangible person who becomes the personification of the process. A 'walking symbol' of change can act as a stimulus to change and can ensure that complacency is avoided.

Second, in many cases, the change agent will be engaged because he or she is an expert in the field. They may have overseen the same change process in many other organisations and so be well acquainted with the usual problems and how to solve them.

Third, the appointment of a change agent sometimes means that senior management time need not be fully occupied with the change process. The responsibility for the change is delegated to the change agent and management thus gain the normal advantages of delegation. Accordingly, senior management are freed up to concentrate on developing future strategy.

4

INTERNATIONAL AND GLOBAL STRATEGIES FOR TRAVEL AND TOURISM ORGANISATIONS

INTRODUCTION

One of the most important considerations in the implementation of strategy is the extent to which the organisation's activities are spread across geographical regions. Some organisations are entirely domestically based, others operate in many countries, and others still operate in almost all regions of the world. This chapter is concerned with a discussion of the key issues surrounding the *why* and *how* questions: why do organisations expand in this way and how do they go about it? The *why* questions are covered in a discussion of the factors that drive increased internationalisation. The *how* questions are answered in a discussion of the market entry options.

LEARNING OBJECTIVES

After studying this chapter, students should be able to:

- define and distinguish between internationalisation and globalisation;
- explain the factors that drive globalisation;
- describe and demonstrate the application of Yip's framework for analysing the extent of globalisation in an industry and market;

- explain the major global strategy alternatives;
- describe the international market entry strategies.

Internationalisation and Globalisation

What is the Difference?

Business has been international since the days of the ancient Egyptians, Phoenicians and Greeks. Merchants travelled the known world to sell products manufactured in their home country and to return with products from other countries. Initially, international business simply took the form of exporting and importing. The term *international* describes any business, which carries out some of its activities across national boundaries.

Globalisation, on the other hand, is more than simply internationalisation. A large multinational company is not necessarily a global business. In order for a business to become global in its operations, we would usually expect a number of important characteristics to be in place.

1. First, global organisations take advantage of the increasing trend towards a convergence of customer needs and wants across international borders (e.g. for fast foods, soft drinks, consumer electronics, hotel accommodation, etc. – see Levitt, 1983).
2. Second, global organisations compete in industries that are globalised. In some sectors, successful competition necessitates a presence in almost every part of the world in order to compete effectively in its global market.
3. Third, global organisations can – and do – locate their value adding activities to those places in the world where the greatest competitive advantages can be made. This might mean, for example, shifting certain operations to a low cost region.
4. Finally, global organisations are able to integrate and coordinate their international activities between countries. The mentality of 'home base, foreign interests' that has been so prevalent amongst

traditional multinational companies is eroded in the culture of global businesses. They have learned effectively to manage and control the various parts of the business across national borders and despite local cultural differences.

The development of an organisation's global strategy, therefore, will be concerned with global competences, global marketing and global configuration and coordination of its value adding activities.

Key concepts: Multinational and Transnational Companies

Both multinationals and transnational companies share the feature that they are usually large and they have direct investments in one or more foreign countries. The foreign investments may be part-shareholdings, but are more usually wholly owned subsidiaries.

The difference is in the degree to which the foreign investments are coordinated. We tend to think of a *transnational* company as one that has a high degree of coordination in its international interests. It will usually have a strategic centre, which manages the global operation such that all parts act in accordance with a centrally managed strategic purpose.

The term *multinational* company is usually taken to mean an international company whose foreign interests are not coordinated from a strategic centre.

Globalisation of Markets and Industries

Levitt and Market Homogenisation

It was Levitt (1983) who first argued that changes in technology, societies, economies and politics are producing a 'global village'. By this he meant that consumer needs in many previously separate national markets were becoming increasingly similar throughout the world. Developments in transport have not only made it easier to move products and materials between countries but they have also resulted in a huge increase in the amount that people travel around the world. Such travel educates people to the products and services available in other countries and, on their return home, they often wish to have access to products and services from overseas. This trend has been reinforced by changes in information technology, particularly those related to cinema and television, which have been important in some aspects of cultural convergence. The development of the World Trade Organisation WTO (not to be confused with the other 'WTO' – the World Tourism Organisation) and its predecessor, GATT (the General Agreement on Tariffs and Trade), has resulted in huge reductions in the barriers to trade between countries since the Second World War. Rising income levels throughout many parts of the world have also given economic impetus to the development of global markets.

It is not only markets which are in many cases becoming more global. Industries are also becoming more global. The value chains of businesses in many industries span the globe. In the case of a diversified tour operator for example, inputs in the form of destinations may be sourced from many parts of the world with the supply from one country varying from year to year based on the costs of the destination relative to other competing destinations. Organisations concentrate certain of their activities in locations where they hope to obtain cost, quality or other advantages. Other activities, like distribution, are also often dispersed around the world. The way that a business configures its activities across national borders can be an important source of competitive advantage. The spread of an organisation's value adding activities around the world also means that there are important advantages to be gained from effective integration and coordination of activities.

Porter and Multi-domesticity

Porter (1990) argued that industries can be either global or *multi-domestic*. Multi-domestic industries are those where competition in each nation is essentially independent. He gives the example of consumer banking where a bank's domestic reputation and resources in one nation have tended to have little effect on its success in other countries. The international banking industry is, Porter argued, essentially a collection of domestic industries.

Global industries are those in which competition is global. The consumer electronics industry is a good example where companies like Philips, Sony and Panasonic compete in almost all countries of the world. The implication would appear to be that businesses should adopt a global strategy in global industries and a multi-local strategy in multi-domestic markets. Yet the situation is not so simple as this. Even markets like consumer banking are becoming more global. The trend is for most industries to become more global, but even within industries major differences may occur.

One way of viewing globalisation is as a continuum from globalisation through international to local or multi-domestic (as shown in Figure 4.1). In travel and tourism the large computer reservations systems have a global reach, whereas towards the other end of the continuum most retail travel agents and rail and bus operators might be viewed as multi-domestic in their orientation. Large airlines often like to portray themselves as 'global' carriers, but close inspection of their route networks reveals that no carrier serves all parts of the world and even in those countries which are served, it is usually only the largest city that is served. Similarly, the large international hotel chains have expanded to include many countries but rarely penetrate local markets beyond the capital city. By way of contrast, the major soft drinks brands such as CocaCola are widely available throughout the world, and are widely dispersed within individual countries.

It is also the case that the degree of globalisation of an industry or market may not be uniform. In other words, some aspects of an industry or market may be indicative of globalisation while others may be indicative of localisation. The degree of globalisation of an industry can be assessed using Yip's globalisation driver framework (1992). This is a more useful framework than Porter's because it makes it possible to evaluate both the overall degree of globalisation

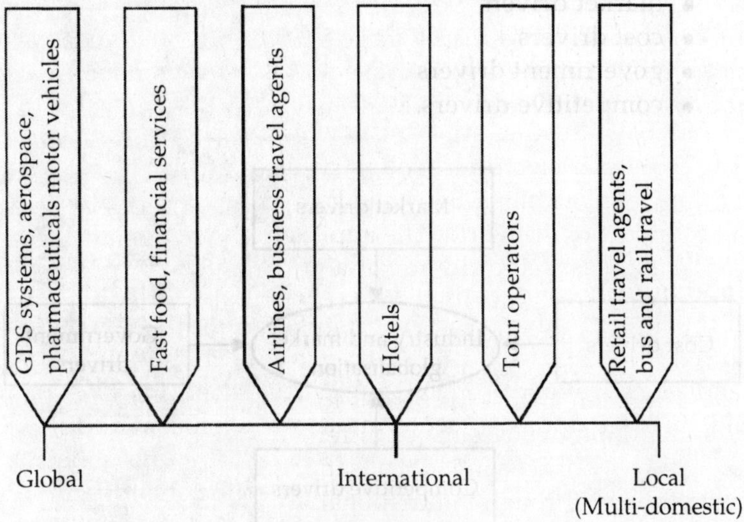

Figure 4.1: Gobal–local continuum.

of an industry and which features of the industry are more or less global in nature.

Globalisation Drivers

Yip's Framework

Yip (1992) argues that it is not simply the case that industries are 'global' or 'not global', rather that they can be global in some respects and not in others. Yip's globalisation driver framework makes it possible to identify which aspects of an industry are global and which aspects differ locally. Analysis using this framework can play an important role in shaping the global strategy of a business. A global strategy, according to Yip, will be global in many respects but may also include features that are locally oriented.

Yip argued that, 'to achieve the benefits of globalisation, the managers of a worldwide business need to recognise when industry conditions provide the opportunity to use global strategy levers'. Yip identified four drivers (Figure 4.2) which determine the nature and extent of globalisation in an industry. These are:

- market drivers
- cost drivers
- government drivers
- competitive drivers.

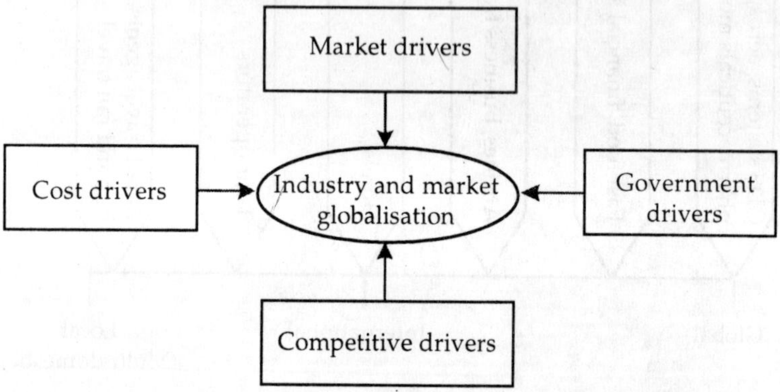

Figure 4.2: A framework describing drivers for internationalisation.

We will consider each of these drivers in turn.

Breakdown of Globalisation Drivers

Market globalisation drivers

- common customer needs
- global customers
- global distribution channels
- transferable marketing techniques
- presence in lead countries

Cost globalisation drivers

- global scale economies
- steep experience curve effect
- sourcing efficiencies
- differences in country costs (including exchange rates)
- high product development costs fast changing technology

Government globalisation drivers

- favourable trade policies
- common marketing regulations
- government owned competitors and customers
- compatible technical standards and common marketing regulations
- host government concerns

Competitive globalisation drivers

- high exports and imports
- competitors from different continents
- interdependence of countries
- competitors globalised

Market Globalisation Drivers

The degree of globalisation of a market will depend upon the extent to which there are common customer needs, global customers, global distribution channels, transferable marketing and lead countries. It is not simply a case of a market being global or not global. Managers must seek to establish which, if any, aspects of their market are global.

Common Customer Needs

Probably the single most important market globalisation driver is the extent to which customers in different countries share the same need or want for a product. The extent of shared need will depend upon cultural, economic, climatic, legal and other similarities and differences. There are numerous examples of markets where customer needs are becoming more similar. Examples include motor vehicles, soft drinks, fast food, but also beach and ski resorts, cruise ships and business travel. The importance of American Express and Carlson Wagonlit in international business travel and the various international hospitality brands operated by Marriott Corporation as well as McDonald's, Burger King and Pizza Hut in fast food, or CocaCola and Pepsi Cola in soft drinks, are all illustrative of converging customer needs in certain markets. Levitt (1983) referred to this similarity of tastes and preference as increasing *market homogenisation* – all markets demanding the same products, regardless of their domestic culture and traditional preferences.

Global Customers and Channels

Global customers purchase products or services in a coordinated way from the best global sources. Yip identifies two types of global customers:

1. *National global customers* – customers who seek the best suppliers in the world and then use the product or service in one country, e.g. a theme park operator might seek the best rides from many countries which are known for providing such engineering skills such as Germany, Switzerland, USA and Japan.

2. *Multinational global customers* – they similarly seek the best suppliers in the world but then use the product or service obtained in many countries, e.g. cruise lines source their ships from many countries such as Finland, France, Germany, Italy and Japan to ensure optional quality standards delivered at a competitive price.

Alongside global customers there are sometimes global, or more often regional, distribution channels, which serve the global customers. Global customers and channels will contribute towards the development of a global market.

Transferable Marketing

Transferable marketing describes the extent to which elements of the marketing mix like brand names and promotions can be used globally without local adaptations. Clearly, when adaptation is not required, it is indicative of a global market. In this way brands like McDonald's, CocaCola and Nike are used globally, and increasingly travel brands such as Hilton, Thomas Cook and Lufthansa also have global recognition. Yet advertising for such brands can be both global and locally adapted according the prevailing attitudes in local markets. If marketing is transferable it will favour a global market.

Lead Countries

When, as Porter (1990) found, there are certain countries that lead in particular industries, then, 'it becomes critical for global competitors to participate in these lead countries in order to be exposed to the sources of innovation'. Lead countries are those that are ahead in product and/or process innovation in their industry. These lead countries help to produce global standards and hence global industries and markets. The USA would clearly been seen as the lead country in terms of Internet travel distribution systems and different hotel formats for example, whilst Germany has taken a lead in developing vertically and horizontally diversified leisure travel companies.

Cost Globalisation Drivers

The potential to reduce costa by global configuration of value adding activities is an important spur towards the globalisation of certain industries. If there are substantial cost advantages to be obtained then an industry will tend to be global.

Global Scale Economies

When an organisation serves a global market then it is able to gain much greater economies of scale than if it serves only domestic or regional markets. Similarly, serving global markets also gives considerable potential for economies of scope. Thus, internationally diversified travel companies such as Air France or Disney who market their activities in many countries gain large economies of scope in product development, marketing, procurement and financing.

KEY CONCEPTS: ECONOMIES OF SCALE AND SCOPE

Economies of scale describe the benefits that are gained when increasing volume results in lower unit costs. Although economies of scale can arise in all parts of the value chain, it is probably best understood by illustrating it using purchasing as an example. An individual purchasing one hotel room will pay more *per item* than a large company contracting to purchase hundreds of hotel rooms to provide for their customers for the season. It is said that the purchaser who is able to purchase in bulk (because of the size and structure of the buyer) enjoys scale economies over smaller organisations that buy in at lower volumes.

An economy of scope is a concept that describes the benefits that can arise in one product or market area as a result of activity in another. Another way of putting it is that the cost of providing two distinct offers from the same organisation is less than providing both separately. Thus, if a tour operator expands to market its activities in another country, the costs of the marketing activity can be shared with the activity in the countries in which it already operates through joint advertising, promotion and so on.

Steep Experience Curve Effect

When there is a steep learning curve in operations and marketing, businesses serving global markets will tend to obtain the greatest benefits. In many service industries there are steep learning curves yielding the greatest benefits to global businesses. Experience and good practices from one country can be shared with other countries and regions thereby increasing organisational learning and experience. Those organisations that are able to communicate the lessons from their experience, i.e. learning, around the organisation quickly and effectively, are likely to be the most successful in global markets. For a hotel group expanding internationally, it is crucial that they get their market entry strategy right. However, experience of entering other country markets will help them make the correct decisions when they choose to enter subsequent markets.

Sourcing Efficiencies

If there are efficiency gains to be made by centralised sourcing carried out globally then this will drive an industry towards globalisation. Businesses like those in sports apparel and fashion clothing benefit from global sourcing to obtain lowest prices and highest quality standards, but this may also apply to cruise lines and airlines seeking crew.

Favourable Logistics

If transportation costs comprise a relatively high proportion of sales value, there will be every incentive to concentrate production in few, large facilities. If transport costs are relatively small, such as with consumer electronic goods, production can be located in several (or many) locations, which are chosen on the basis of other cost criteria such as land or labour costs.

Differences in Country Costs

Operational costs (building, labour, etc.) vary from country to country which can stimulate globalisation. Thus, countries with lower operational costs will tend to attract businesses to locate activities in the country. Many Asian countries have attracted international hotel chains because of their favourable cost conditions. Although countries like Thailand have suffered in some respects because of the devaluation of their currency in 1997–98, from the point of view of being chosen as tourist centres, they have benefited.

Fast Changing Technology and High Product Development Costs

Product life cycles are shortening as the pace of technological change increases. At the same time research and development costs are increasing in many industries. Such product development costs can only be recouped by high sales in global markets. Domestic markets simply do not yield the volumes of sales required to cover high R&D costs. Thus, industries like pharmaceuticals and automobiles as well as cruising and airlines face very rapidly changing technology and hyper competition, together with high development and equipment purchase costs. As a consequence they must operate in global markets so as to ensure the volumes of sales necessary to recoup these costs.

Government Globalisation Drivers

Since the Second World War many governments have taken individual and collective action to reduce barriers to global trade.

Favourable Trade Policies

The World Trade Organisation and its predecessor, the General Agreement on Tariffs and Trade, have done much to reduce barriers to trade, which have, in the past, hindered globalisation of many industries. Although there are still significant barriers to trade in certain areas, the movement towards freedom of trade has been substantial, thus favouring globalisation. The growth of customs unions and 'single markets' such as the European Union and the North American Free Trade Area (NAFTA) have also made an important contribution in this regard. In the airline industry deregulation occurred in the USA in 1978 and was followed by Europe in the 1990s.

Compatible Technical Standards and Common Marketing Regulations

Many of the differences in technical standards between countries, which hindered globalisation in the past, have been reduced. For example, telecommunications standards, which have traditionally differed between countries, are increasingly being superseded by international standards. Similarly standards are converging in the pharmaceutical, airline and computing industries, which make it easier to produce globally accepted products.

There remain important differences in advertising regulations between countries, with the UK regulations among the strictest. Generally, however, these differences are being eroded and this is expected to favour greater globalisation.

Government Owned Competitors and Customers

Government owned competitors, who often enjoy state subsidies, can act as a stimulus to globalisation as they frequently compete with other global competitors, thus being forced to become more efficient and global market oriented. On the other hand, government-owned customers tend to favour domestic suppliers, which can act as a barrier to globalisation. The privatisation of many state-owned businesses in many European countries (and elsewhere in the world) has reduced this barrier to globalisation.

Host Government Concerns

The attitudes and policies of host government concerns can either hinder or favour globalisation. In certain circumstances, host governments may favour the entry of global businesses into domestic industries and markets, which will assist globalisation. For example, the Malaysian government has, in recent years, done much to attract inward investment by Japanese, American and European-based hotel companies. The more governments that espouse such policies, the greater will be globalisation of an industry. In other cases, host governments will seek to protect industries which they see as strategically important and will attempt to prevent foreign businesses from entry. Thus, many countries such as the USA limit the ownership of American airlines by foreign companies and restrict access to foreign airlines for domestic airline routes.

Competitive Globalisation Drivers

The greater the strength of the competitive drivers the greater will be the tendency for an industry to globalise. Global competition in an industry will become more intense when:

- there is a high level of trade between countries;
- the competitors in the industry are widely spread (they will often be on different continents):
- the economies of the countries involved are interdependent;
- competitors in the industry are already globalised.

High Exports and Imports

The higher the level of trade in products and services between countries the greater will be the pressure for globalisation of an industry.

Competitors from Different Continents

The more countries that are represented in an industry and the more widely spread they are, the greater the likelihood of globalisation.

Interdependence of Countries

If national economies are already relatively interdependent, then this will act as a stimulus for increased globalisation. Such interdependence may arise through, for example, multiple trading links in other industries, through being a part of a single market or through being in a shared political alliance

Competitors Globalised

If a competitor is already globalised and employing a global strategy then there will be pressure on other businesses in the industry to globalise as well. Globalisation in the business travel sector is high because of the pressure on organisations to compete globally. Business travel agents are often required to serve the needs of their customers who themselves are global companies. Such companies often wish to deal with one organisation, which is able to service its travel needs on a global basis.

Using the Globalisation Driver Framework

Yip's globalisation driver framework provides an extremely useful tool for analysing the degree of globalisation of an industry or market. Equally, it makes possible an understanding of which particular aspects of an industry or market are global and which aspects are localised. Each of the drivers must be analysed for the industry and market under consideration and the results of the analysis will play an important role in assisting managers to form the global strategy of their organisation. The results will help to determine which features of the strategy are globally standardised and which features are locally adapted.

There are several models that explain the basis of global strategy. This chapter explains the frameworks developed by Porter (1986a, 1990) and Yip (1992). Porter focuses on adapting the generic strategy framework to global conditions and the role of configuration and coordination of value adding activities in securing global competitive advantage. Yip develops the concept of 'Total Global Strategy' based upon his globalisation driver framework.

Although these are the models considered in this chapter, interested readers should consider reading the work of Bartlett and Ghoshal (1987, 1989), Prahalad and Doz (1987), Ellis and Williams (1995) and Stonehouse *et al.* (1999). There is also a large developing literature on globalisation and its impacts on the travel and tourism industry. See, for example, Go and Pine (1995), Hanlon (1996), Keller (1996), Knowles (2001), Wahab and Cooper (2001).

Porter's Global Generic Strategies

Porter (1980) argued that competitive advantage rests upon an organisation selecting and adopting one of the three generic strategies (differentiation, cost leadership or focus) to modify the five competitive forces in its favour so as to earn higher profits than the industry average. In 1986 Porter extended the generic strategy framework to global business. The model suggests that a business operating in international markets has five strategy alternatives (Figure 4.3). The five strategic postures are defined according to their position in respect to two intersecting continua: the extent to which the industry is globalised (or country-centred horizontal axis) and the breadth of the segments served by the competitors in an industry (which, put simply, means the number of different customer groups served by an industry).

The five strategic postures are described below.

1. *Global cost leadership* – the business seeks to be the lowest cost producer of a product globally. Globalisation provides the opportunity for high volume sales and greater economies of scale and scope than domestic competitors.

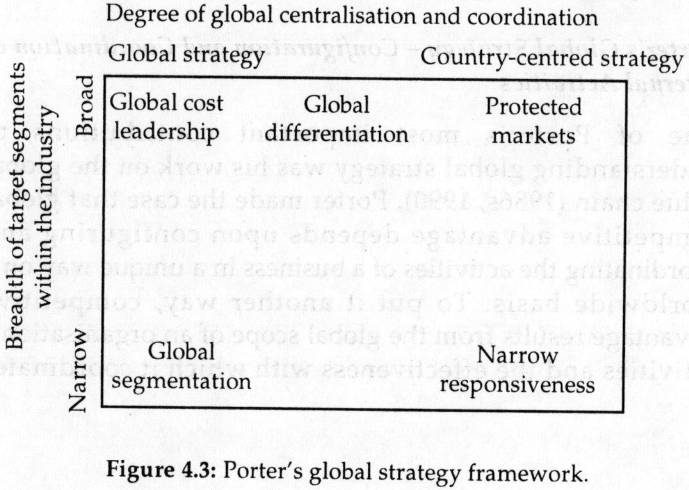

Figure 4.3: Porter's global strategy framework.

2. *Global differentiation* – the business seeks to differentiate products and services globally, often on the basis of a global brand name.
3. *Global segmentation* – this is the global variant of a focus strategy when a single market segment is targeted on a worldwide basis employing either cost leadership or differentiation.
4. *Protected markets* – a business identifies national markets where its particular business is favoured or protected by the host government.
5. *National responsiveness* – the business adapts its strategy to meet the distinctive needs of local markets (i.e. not a global strategy). Suitable for purely domestic businesses.

The model suffers from similar flaws relating to the generic strategy framework. As in the case of the conventional understanding of generic strategy, it is possible for a business to pursue a hybrid international strategy. Expedia.com, the online travel product distributor, for example, concentrates on both cost control (with regard to its supplier) and also on ensuring that it differentiates its products on the basis of reliability of delivery and the scope of its operations.

Porter's Global Strategy – Configuration and Coordination of Internal Activities

One of Porter's most important contributions to understanding global strategy was his work on the global value chain (1986s, 1990). Porter made the case that global competitive advantage depends upon configuring and coordinating the activities of a business in a unique way on a worldwide basis. To put it another way, competitive advantage results from the global scope of an organisation's activities and the effectiveness with which it coordinates

Coordination of activities	Configuration of activities: Geographically dispersed	Configuration of activities: Geographically concentrated
High	High degree of dispersal of activities with a high degree of coordination among subsidiaries.	Purest global strategy (high degree of concentration of activities and coordination).
Low	Country-centred strategy for company with several national subsidiaries, each operating in only one country. Activity dispersed and little coordination.	Strategy based upon exporting of product with decentralised marketing in each host country – activities concentrated but not coordinated.

Figure 4.4: Configuration and coordination for international strategy.

them. Porter (1986a, 1990) argued that global competitive advantage depends upon two sets of decisions:

1. *Configuration of value adding activities* – managers must decide in which nations they will carry out each of the activities in the value chain of their business. Configuration can be broad (involving many countries) of narrow (few or one countries).
2. *Coordination of value adding activities* – managers must decide the most effective way of coordinating value adding activities, which are carried out in different parts of the world.

Configuration and coordination present four broad alternatives, illustrated in Figure 4.4. In the case of configuration, an organisation can choose to disperse its activities to a range of locations around the world or it may choose to concentrate key activities in locations that present certain advantages. Many businesses concentrate the manufacture of their products in countries where costs are low but skill levels are good. Many call centres are located in

India where labour costs are low but the workforce is skilled, motivated and flexible. An organisation can decide to coordinate its worldwide activities or to mange them locally in each part of the world. The latter approach misses the opportunity for global management economies of scale. For Porter, the 'purest global strategy' is when an organisation concentrates key activities in locations giving competitive advantages and coordinates activities on a global basis. In the long-term, according to Porter, organisations should move towards 'purest global strategy' as far as is practicable.

'Total' Global Strategy

Yip's Stages in Total Global Strategy

Yip (1992) argued that successful global strategy must be based upon a comprehensive globalisation analysis of the drivers we encountered above. Managers of a global business must, he contends, evaluate the globalisation drivers for their industry and market and must formulate their global strategy on the basis of this analysis. If, for example, they find that customer demand is largely homogeneous for their product then they can produce a largely standardised product for sale throughout the world. If, on the other hand, they find that there are few cost advantages of global concentration of operations because of adverse economies of scale or scope, they may choose to disperse their operational activities around the world to be close to their customers in different parts of the world. Thus, the 'total global strategy' of an organisation can be a mix of standardisation and local adaptation as market and industry conditions dictate.

Yip went on to identify three stages in developing a 'total global strategy'.

1. *Developing a core strategy* – this will, in effect, involve building core competences and generic or hybrid strategy which can potentially give global competitive advantage.
2. *Internationalising the core strategy* – this will be the stage at which the core competences and generic strategy are

introduced to international markets and when the organisation beings to locate its value adding activities in locations where competitive advantages like low cost access to resources are available. This will include choice of which markets the business will enter and the means by which it will enter them.

3. *Globalising the international strategy* – this stage is based upon coordinating and integrating the core competences and strategy on a global basis. It will also include deciding which elements of the strategy are to be standardised and which are to be locally adapted on the basis of the strength of the globalisation drivers in the industry and market.

Key Strategic Decisions

Once a business has developed core competences and strategies which can potentially be exploited globally, the decisions must be made as to where and how to employ them. Initial moves into overseas markets will involve market development as such markets and segments can be regarded as new to the business. The initial market development may then be followed by product development and, perhaps, diversification.

When a business enters international and global markets it will be necessary to build new competences, alongside those that have brought about domestic competitive advantage. These new competences could well be in the areas of global sourcing and logistics and global management.

The globalisation of a business does not happen overnight. It may well involve entry to key countries with the largest markets first, followed by entry to less important countries later. In the initial stages of globalisation the key decisions are usually as follows:

- Which countries are to be entered first?
- In which countries are value adding activities to be located?
- Which market development strategies are to be employed to gain entry to chosen overseas markets?

Market Entry Decisions

Decision Criteria

The decision as to which countries and markets are to be entered first will be based upon a number of important factors.

- *The potential size of the market* – is the market for the product in the country likely to be significant? This will, in turn, be determined by the factors following.
- *Economic factors* – are income levels adequate to ensure that significant numbers of people are likely to be able to afford the product?
- *Cultural and linguistic factors* – is the culture of the country likely to favour acceptance of the product to be offered?
- *Political factors* – what are the factors that may limit entry to markets in the host country?
- *Technological factors* – are levels of technology adequate to support provision of the product in the host market and are technological standards compatible?

To begin with a business will choose to enter markets in those countries where the above conditions are most favourable.

Location of Value Adding Activities

Managers must determine within which countries they will locate key value adding activities of their business. They will seek to gain cost, skill and resource advantages. In other words, they will attempt to locate activities in countries where there are production advantages to be gained.

Such advantages depend upon:

- *wage levels* – low wage levels will assist in low production costs;
- *skill levels* – there must be suitably skilled labour available;
- *availability of materials* – suitable materials must be accessible;

- *infrastructure* – transport and communications must be favourable to the logistics of the business.

The existence of these conditions within a country will, in turn, depend upon:

- *economic factors* – level of economic development, wage levels, exchange rate conditions;
- *social factors* – attitudes to work, levels of education and training;
- *political factors* – legislation favouring investment etc.;
- *technological factors* – levels of technology, and transport and communications infrastructure of the country.

Market Development Methods

Once decisions have been made as to which countries' markets are to be entered and where value adding activities are to be located, the task for management becomes the determination of which method of development to employ to enter another country. Broadly speaking, a business can choose either *internal or external methods for development* of overseas markets. Internal methods are usually slower, but tend to entail lower risk. External methods involve the business developing relationships with other businesses. Internal methods of development include direct exporting, overseas sourcing of suppliers, local processing and establishing overseas subsidiaries. External methods include joint ventures and alliances, mergers and acquisitions, franchising and licensing. The choice of method will depend upon a number of factors:

- the size of the investment required or the amount of investment capital available;
- knowledge of the country to be entered and potential risk involved (e.g. of political instability);
- revenue and cash flow forecasts and expectations;
- operating cost considerations;
- control considerations (some investment options will have implications for the parent to control activity in the host country).

Internal Development Methods

Internal methods are based upon the organisation exploiting its own resources and competences and involve the organisation carrying out some of its activities overseas. This may be exporting its products or setting up some form of production facilities abroad. The advantages of internal methods of development are that they maximize future revenue from sales abroad and they make possible a high degree of control over overseas activities. On the other hand, they can involve significant risk if knowledge of the host country and its markets are limited, and they may require considerable direct investment from the business.

The major internal methods of development overseas are direct exporting and development of overseas facilities.

Direct Exporting

Direct exporting is the transfer of services across national borders from the home operation. The service may simply be provided from the home country. For example, a cruise line might advertise its products in a particular country but the line might not have any staff in that country. Instead customers are directed to a sales office in the cruise line's home country. As sales increase, a sales office may be set up in the overseas country.

To avoid some of the pitfalls of direct exporting (like lack of local knowledge and access to distribution channels), many exporting businesses make use of local sales agents or distribute their products (often known as a *piggyback* distribution arrangement).

Overseas Operations

Organisations may choose to offer their products themselves directly in foreign countries. There are a number of reasons for such direct investment. The investment allows the company to gain local knowledge, to maintain control over the operations and to tailor the products and marketing to local demands. Relationships can also be forged with local suppliers and government, which might be helpful in developing the business.

Internal development may involve establishing a foreign subsidiary of the business. This is the case when it is favourable for the parent company to have total control of its overseas operations, decision-making and profits. Such a subsidiary may carry out the full range of activities of the parent business or it may be only an operational or marketing subsidiary.

External Development Methods

External methods of development involve the organisation entering into relationships with businesses in a host country. External development methods can take the form of alliances or joint ventures, mergers or acquisitions, or franchises. Such methods have the advantages of providing local knowledge, potentially reducing risks, and reducing investment costs (except in the case of mergers or acquisitions). The major disadvantages (again except in the case of mergers and acquisitions) are reduced revenues and reduced control of activities as optimal income is traded off against the advantage of lower financial exposure.

International Alliances and Joint Ventures

Alliances and joint ventures allow a business to draw upon the skills, local knowledge, resources and competences of a locally based company. They reduce the risks of entry to overseas markets by providing local knowledge and help reduce investment costs.

International Mergers and Acquisitions

A business may use mergers or acquisitions to enter overseas markets. Such mergers and acquisitions give a business access to the knowledge, resources and competences of a business based in the host country thus reducing some of the risks of market entry.

International Franchising and Licensing

A franchise is an arrangement under which a franchiser supplies a franchisee with a tried-and-tested brand name, products and expertise in return for the payment of a proportion of profits or sales. The major advantage to the franchiser is that the risk, investment and operating costs of entering overseas markets are reduced considerably. At the same time the franchisee can contribute their local knowledge whilst also benefiting from the lower risks associated with an established business idea. Much of Burger King and Holiday Inn, or the Choice hotel expansion in overseas markets for example have come through franchise development.

5

STRATEGIC MANAGEMENT – PRESENT AND FUTURE TRENDS

INTRODUCTION

In travel and tourism, as in other industrial sectors, managers are learning that adopting a strategic and holistic approach to management can benefit organisational competitiveness. However, strategic management is not a mature discipline, if indeed it can be called a discipline when it is in fact a multi- and inter-disciplinary field of study. Strategists draw heavily upon disciplines as diverse as organisation theory and behaviour, human resource management, economics, accounting and finance, and marketing as well as attempting to formulate their own theories and analytical frameworks. The future of strategic management will undoubtedly be longer than its past. For this reason the theories, tools and techniques employed in strategic management in many cases are far from fully formulated. The subject will continue to evolve and the sophistication of its methods and methodology will develop and improve over time.

At the heart of strategic management is the desire to explain why certain organisations achieve competitive advantage through superior performance. The view in the 1980s was that competitive advantage was based upon the competitive positioning of the organisation in its environment based upon highly systematic planning (Argenti, 1965; Porter, 1980, 1985). This view has since been challenged by strategists who believe that in a turbulent business environment, strategy can be developed incrementally and that competitive advantage depends upon the ability of the business to build core competences that cannot be easily replicated by competitors (Prahalad and Hamel, 1990; Kay, 1993; Hamel and Prahalad 1994; Heene and Sanchez, 1997). This chapter, intended to be a summary of the book, serves the dual purpose of identifying the origins of strategic management before considering recent developments which will shape its future.

Learning Objectives

After studying this chapter, students should be able to:

- outline the development of strategic management as an academic discipline;
- explain and explore the planned/prescriptive approach to strategic management;
- explain and explore the emergent/incremental approach to strategic management;
- explain and explore the competitive positioning approach to strategic management;
- explain and explore the resource/core competence approach to strategic management;
- identify likely developments in strategic management, namely collaborative advantage and knowledge management.

Themes in Strategic Management

The 'Big' Controversies

The developing nature of strategy as a coherent academic discipline is reflected in two related debates revolving around what constitutes the most appropriate approach to strategic management (Figure 5.1). There is some disagreement among strategists on the best way of understanding the determinants of competitive advantage. Some writers advocate an approach to strategic management which is *planned* or *prescriptive*

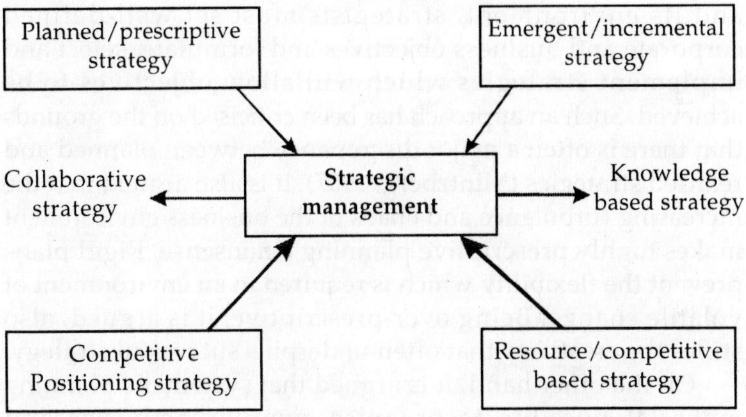

Figure 5.1: The development of strategic management.

(sometimes called *deliberate*) while others argue that it is better to evolve strategy incrementally (the *emergent* approach to strategy. A parallel debate centres upon whether competitive advantage stems primarily from the competitive position of the business in its industry or from business-specific core competences. These themes are explored in the following sections of this chapter.

The debate surrounding the development of strategic management can be summarised under two broad headings:

1. The planned/prescriptive versus emergent/incremental controversy.
2. The competitive positioning versus resource/core competence based strategy controversy.

We summarise the main features of these approaches and briefly explore their advantages and disadvantages (see Table 5.1). The arguments are discussed below.

The Prescriptive versus Emergent Strategy Debate

Planned or Prescriptive Strategy

The planned or prescriptive approach views the formulation and implementation of strategic management as a logical, rational and systematic process. After analysis of the business and its environment, strategists must set well-defined corporate and business objectives and formulate, select and implement strategies which will allow objectives to be achieved. Such an approach has been criticised on the grounds that there is often a major discrepancy between planned and realised strategies (Mintzberg, 1987). It is also argued that the increasing turbulence and chaos of the business environment makes highly prescriptive planning a nonsense. Rigid plans prevent the flexibility which is required in an environment of volatile change. Being over-prescriptive, it is argued, also stifles the creativity that often underpins successful strategy.

On the other hand, it is argued that systematic planning makes it possible to organise complex activities and information, unite business objectives, set targets against which performance can be evaluated and generally increases the degree of control which can be exercised over the operation of the business. The planned or prescriptive approach is often linked to the *competitive positioning* approach (see later in this chapter).

Emergent or Incremental Strategy

The emergent or incremental view of strategy adopts the position that strategy must be evolved incrementally over time. This view is based upon the premise that businesses are complex social organisations operating in rapidly changing environments. Under such circumstances, strategy will tend to evolve as a result of the interaction between stakeholder groups and between the business and its environment. It is argued that an emergent approach has the advantages of increased organisational flexibility. It can form a basis in organisational learning and can provide an internal culture for managers to think and act creatively rather than have to act within the rigid framework of deliberate strategy. The danger is that an emergent approach may result in a lack of purpose in strategy and it can make it difficult to evaluate performance (because if an organisation has no explicit objective, performance against it cannot be measured).

Table 5.1: Approaches to Strategic Management.

Approach	*Theory*	*Advantages*	*Criticisms*
Prescriptive or planning strategy.	Strategic management is a highly formalised planning process.	Clear objectives provide focus for the business.	There are often major, discrepancies between planned and realised strategy.
	Business objectives are set and strategies are formulated and implemented to achieve them.	Objectives can be translated into targets against which performance can be measured and monitored.	Rigid planning in a dynamic and turbulent business environment can be unproductive.
		Resources can be allocated to specific objectives and efficiency can be judged.	Prescriptions can stifle creativity.
		The approach is logical and rational.	Rigid adherence to plans may mean missed business opportunities.
Emergent or incremental strategy.	Strategy emerges and develops incrementally over time in the absence of rigid planning.	Emergent strategy increases flexibility in a turbulent environment allowing the business to respond to threats and exploit opportunities.	There is a danger of 'strategic drift' as objectives lack clarity.
		Changing stakeholder interactions can mean that strategy is often, of necessity, emergent.	It is more difficult to evaluate performance as targets are less well defined.
Competitive positioning	Competitive advantage results	Well-developed analytical frame-	Neglects the importance of business-

Approach	*Theory*	*Advantages*	*Criticisms*
approach to strategy.	from an organisation's position in respect to its industry.	works like Porter's five forces, value chain and generic strategies.	specific competences as opposed to industry wide factors.
	The business analyses the strength of the competitive forces in its industry and selects an appropriate generic strategy. The business configures its value adding activities to support this generic strategy.	Structured approach helps to simplify the complexity of business and the business environment.	Some of the analytical frameworks (e.g. generic strategies) have been widely criticised.
	The approach to strategy is 'outside-in'.	Good for indentifying opportunities and threats in the environment.	
Resource or competence based approach to strategy.	Organisations must identify and build core competences or distinctive capabilities which can be leveraged in a number of markets.	The approach emphasises the importance of the individual business in acquiring competitive advantage.	Analytical frameworks are in their infancy and are currently poorly developed.
	The approach to strategy is 'inside-out'.	Strategic intent, vision and creativity are emphasised.	The importance of the environment in determining competitive advantage is underestimated.

To counter the criticisms of emergent strategy, Quinn (1978) and Quinn and Voyer (1994) see a role for some planning in the context of emergent strategy, advocating 'purposeful incrementalism'. This approach places a strong emphasis on *organisational learning* (see later in this chapter).

The Competitive Positioning versus Resource/Core Competence Debate

Competitive Positioning

This school of thought dominated strategic management in the 1980s and still had considerable significance in the 1990s. Although the approach has now been widely criticised, the analytical frameworks devised by Porter in the 1980s (1980, 1985) are still widely used by both managers and academics. The major strength of the approach lies in the ready applicability of these frameworks to analysis of the business and its environment. The approach to strategy is essentially 'outside-in' to establish a competitive position for the business in its environment which results in its outperforming its rivals.

In terms of procedure, the process of analysing competitive position begins with the *five forces framework.* This is used to analyse the nature of competition in the organisation's industry. This is followed by selection of the appropriate *generic strategy* together with *value chain analysis* to ensure that the business configures its value adding activities in such a way as to support a strategy based on either differentiation or cost leadership.

In the 1990s, this approach was criticised for its overemphasis of the role of the *industry* in determining profitability and its underestimation of the importance of the individual business (Rumelt, 1991), Porter's frameworks have also been criticised as being too static, although Porter argues that they must be applied repeatedly to take account of the dynamism of the environment. The reality is that without Porter's work, strategic management would be devoid of many of its most practical and applicable analytical tools.

Resource or Core Competence Based Strategy

The 1990s witnessed the rise of what is known as *resource* or *core competence based* strategic management (Prahalad and Hamel, 1990; Kay, 1993; Heene and Sanchez, 1997). The major difference to the competitive positioning approach is that the importance of the individual business in achieving competitive advantage is emphasised rather than the industry. The approach is therefore 'inside-out'. Although this approach came to prominence in the 1990s, its origins lie in the work of Penrose (1959), who emphasised the importance of the business and its resources in determining its performance. Interest in the approach was revived by Prahalad and Hamel's 1990 work 'The core competence of the corporation'. A core competence is some combination of resources, skills, knowledge and technology which distinguishes an organisation from its competitors in the eyes of customers. This distinctiveness results in competitive advantage.

The approach also emphasises organisational learning, knowledge management and collaborative business networks as sources of competitive advantage (Demarest, 1997; Sanchez and Heene, 1997).

The resource/core competence approach has focused the search for competitive advantage on the individual business but its critics argue that it lacks the well developed analytical frameworks of the competitive positioning school and, perhaps, understates the potential importance of the business environment in determining success or failure.

Towards an Integrated Approach to Strategy

Similarities and Differences between the Approaches

The prescriptive and competitive positioning approaches are often seen as related to each other because they both adopt a highly structured view of strategic management. Similarly, the emergent and competence based approaches are often linked because of their shared focus on organisational knowledge and learning.

On the other hand, the prescriptive and emergent approaches are often presented as being diametrically opposed, as are the competitive positioning and competence based approaches. The reality is that the approaches are in many ways complementary as they present different perspectives of the same situation.

Mintzberg, Quinn and Ghoshal (1995) argue that the competence based and competitive positioning approaches ought be seen as 'complementary, representing two different forms of analysis both of which must be brought to bear for improving the quality of strategic thinking and analysis'. Similarly, Quinn and Voyer (1994) recognise that within logical incrementalism 'formal planning techniques do serve some essential functions'.

Acknowledging the Contribution of Each Approach

The point is that each approach has its merits. By acknowledging the contribution of each approach, managers can arrive at an enriched method of understanding the complex area of strategic management. The contribution of each approach to an integrated understanding is summarised below.

- *Planned/prescriptive* – a degree of planning is necessary to provide focus for the strategy of the organisation and to assist in the evaluation of performance.
- *Emergent/incremental* – plans must always be flexible to allow organisations to learn and adapt to changes in the environment.
- *Competitive positioning* – emphasises the importance of the environment and provides useful tools for analysing the business in the context of its industry.
- *Resource/competence based* – focuses on the importance of the business and assists in identifying company-specific sources of competitive advantage.

Accordingly, we suggest that strategy must be both inward and outward looking, planned and emergent. By adopting this synthesis, a broader understanding of competitive advantage can be gained.

The Future of Strategic Management Thinking

This book has discussed the 'state of the art' in strategic thinking at the beginning of the twenty-first century. In attempting to predict the areas that will focus the minds of academics in the near future, two central areas of interest are prominent – *collaborative advantage* and *knowledge management.*

Collaboration and Competitive Behaviour in Industries

In recent years, considerable research and theorisation has focused on the extent to which collaboration between businesses (as opposed to competition) may contribute towards the attainment of competitive advantage (Contractor and Lorange, 1988; Hamel *et al.*, 1989; Quinn *et al.*, 1990; Reeve, 1990; Davidow and Malone, 1992; Heene and Sanchez., 1997).

Collaboration in Non-core Activities

The competence based approach suggests that businesses should concentrate upon developing core competences so as to achieve competitive advantage. Any activities that are not seen as core can be outsourced to other organisations for whom those activities are core. Most networks centre on a focal business whose strategy drives the operation of the network. Quinn, Doorley and Paquette (1990) suggest that such are the changes in service technologies that they now 'provide sufficient scale economies, flexibility, efficiency and specialisation potentials that outside vendors [sellers] can supply many important corporate functions at greatly enhanced value and lower cost. Thus, many of those functions should be outsourced.'

Rather than abandoning control to outside vendors it is sometimes best to form some sort of alliance or network with them. Collaborative networks potentially provide several advantages by:

- alowing businesses to concentrate on their core competences and core activities;
- allowing businesses to pool core competences, thus creating synergy between them;
- reducing bureaucracy and allowing flatter organisational structures;
- increasing efficiency and reducing costs;
- improving flexibility and responsiveness;

- making it difficult for competitors to imitate.

The formation of a collaborative network will involve:

- identification of the core competences of the organisation;
- identification and focus upon activities which are critical to the core competence of the organisation and outsourcing those which are not;
- achieving the internal and external linkages in the value/supply chain which are necessary for effective coordination of activities and which enhance responsiveness.

Collaboration can be:

- *horizontal* – partners are at the same stage of the value system and are often competitors;
- *vertical* – partners are at different stages of the value system (this includes collaboration with suppliers, distributors and customers).

Collaboration can provide benefits including the linking of core competences (of the two parties in the relationship), access to resources and technology, risk reduction, greater control over supplies, betters access to customers and reduced competition. Collaboration, however, can create problems which include conflicting objectives between the participating businesses, cultural differences, changing requirements among the partners and coordination and integration problems.

Virtual Organisations

Developments in Information and Communications Technology (ICT) have greatly increased the potential for collaboration between businesses by making it much easier to integrate and coordinate network activities. These changes in technology have made possible the development of 'virtual' organisations. A virtual organisation is a network of linked businesses who coordinate and integrate their activities so effectively that they give the appearance of a single business organisation.

There is considerable potential for such virtual organisations to enhance competitive advantage. ICT linkages greatly increase flexibility and efficiency, and make it difficult for competitors to replicate the activities of the network. Linkages to suppliers and customers are greatly improved as are flows of the information required for strategic decision-taking. The net result is that the virtual corporation is more flexible, more responsive and better able than its non-virtual rivals to compete on the bases of time and customer satisfaction.

Organisational Learning and Knowledge Management

Closely related to the rational/logical approaches to strategy (such as the prescriptive and competitive positioning schools of thought) is the notion that organisations must continually learn both about themselves and their environment. At the same time – and here this point is in agreement with the core competence approach – it is widely acknowledged that organisational knowledge underpins many core competences. Accordingly, organisational learning and knowledge management have been the subject of considerable recent research and theorisation (see for example Argyris, 1992; Demarest, 1997; Grant, 1997). Grant (1997) argues that 'the knowledge-based view represents a confluence of a number of streams of research, the most prominent being "resource-based theory" and "epistemology"'.

Explicit and Implicit Knowledge

Organisational learning and knowledge management are concerned with the creation, development and dissemination of knowledge within an organisation. This 'knowledge' can be either explicit or implicit.

- *explicit knowledge* is knowledge whose meaning is clearly stated, details of which can be recorded and stored (such as important formulations, procedures, ways of acting, etc);
- *explicit* or *tacit knowledge* (Demarest, 1997) is often unstated, based upon individual experience and

difficult to record and store. Implicit knowledge is often a vital source of core competence and competitive advantage as it is most difficult for competitors to emulate (such as experience in a given sector, an understanding of a particular technology or the multiple contact networks that have been built up over many years by managers and sales people).

Both forms of knowledge begin as individual knowledge but, to substantially improve performance, they must be transformed into organisational knowledge. This is a particularly difficult transformation for implicit knowledge. It is the role of knowledge management to ensure that individual learning becomes organisational learning.

Types of Organisational Learning

Argyris (Argyris and Schon, 1978; Argyris, 1992) argues that organisations must develop 'double loop learning'. In other words, learning is not just a case of learning how to solve an immediate problem but must also aim at developing principles that will inform and determine future behaviour. It must also result in the ability to generalise from specific learning. Such learning takes place when individual solutions are reached and then generalised to apply in other circumstances.

Senge (1990) identifies two types of learning found in leading organisations: 'adaptive learning' and 'generative learning'. Adaptive learning centres on changing in response to developments in the business environment. Such adaptation is often necessary for business survival. Generative learning is, on the other hand, about building new competences or identifying or creating opportunities for leveraging existing competences in new competitive arenas. For example, the entry of MyTravel plc into the low-cost airline sector in 2002 was based upon leveraging existing competences. The competences related to charter airline operations were complemented by new competences based upon learning about the nature of scheduled air services.

The Keys to Successful Knowledge Management

Knowledge management incorporates organisational learning but it is also concerned with the management of existing stocks of knowledge. Effective knowledge management must overcome:

- barriers to learning and knowledge creation;
- difficulties in storing and sharing knowledge (particularly tacit knowledge);
- difficulties in valuing and measuring knowledge (based on Demarest, 1997).

Knowledge management is, therefore, primarily concerned with the creation of new knowledge, storage and sharing of knowledge and the control of knowledge. Knowledge management is an important element in building core competences, which must be distinctive and difficult to imitate.

The often intangible nature of knowledge tends to make it distinctive and difficult to copy. In the case of a company like Microsoft, it is evident that its core competences are largely knowledge based. Quinn (1992) argues that 'most successful enterprises today can be considered intelligent enterprises' as they focus on building knowledge based core competences. Similarly, Grant (1997) points out that many companies are now developing corporate-wide systems to track, access, exploit and create organisational knowledge. Within such organisations, questioning and creativity are encouraged, as are trust; teamwork and sharing. At the same time, they have created infrastructures which support learning, which assist in the storage and controlled diffusion of knowledge, and which coordinate its application in creating and supporting core competences.

There is some way to go in understanding the role of knowledge and its management in strategy. It is likely that significant developments will take place in this area as the new millennium proceeds.

6

CASE ANALYSIS IN STRATEGIC MANAGEMENT

Introduction

Case study analysis invariably forms a part of most courses in strategic management. Originally developed as a teaching tool in the major American Business Schools, particularly Harvard, case studies are now widely used by most business schools. Case studies are used so as to enable students to understand the complex nature of strategic decision-making and the inter-related nature of such decisions, i.e. a decision taken in one part of a business will have a knock-on effect upon other parts of the business. Although there is perhaps no substitute for management experience in the real world, case studies represent the next best thing.

The case studies you are asked to analyse indicate the broad range of strategic decisions managers need to take in the real world. The cases may vary in a number of ways which may affect the type of analysis that is carried out and the way in which the results of the analysis are presented. Cases may relate to:

- large or small scale organisations;
- organisations that the complex in their structure and management or which are relatively simple to understand;
- organisations with exposure to particular types of risk;
- organisations that are successful or organisations that are in difficulties;

- organisations and their circumstances that are known to you or organisations in which their true circumstances will be changed in order to illustrate particular points;
- organisations that are totally fictitious and created just for illustrative purposes or companies in which the name of the company and the names of managers and so on will be altered so as to disguise the real company being considered;
- organisation activities in the present day or at a date in the past.

In all cases considered, however, it is important to realise that what you are normally being asked to do is to place yourself in the position of a manager of an organisation or within an industry sector at a particular moment in time. The important point is not what actually happened to the company in reality, but given the available information, how would you have made sense of the information available to you at the time and what actions you would have recommended in the circumstances.

Reading and Studying the Case

In considering cases you are expected to go beyond merely describing the circumstances of the case. The case method requires you to analyse the cases in detail and to develop sound, reasoned judgements that will lead to recommendations being made. In so doing it is important to recognise the key or strategic points of the case and to distinguish these points from less substantial or trivial points.

Many cases contain 'red herrings', which are designed to mislead and confuse, and in so doing replicate the real world in which information comes from several directions and reaches managers by different means. A manager has to make sense of the information and discern the important or urgent from the less important or less urgent. So in analysing a case ask yourself, 'What are the central issues in the case?'

There will be instances when you feel that you do not have all the information you need to make the best decision.

The information presented in the case, however, is often incomplete by design and again reflects the situation pertaining in the real world. Managers often have to make decisions based on the information available to them at the time, and although they might wish they had further information, it is either unavailable or not available within the necessary time-scale with the resources available. Thus, you are required to make the best possible use of the information that you actually have at your disposal.

You are also asked to make your analysis at the time of the case. Managers do not have the benefit of hindsight when managing their companies (much as they might want it), they have to manage with the information available to them at that time and so it is with case studies. A tour operation set in 2000 would not have known, for instance, of the terrorist attacks on America in September 2001 and its subsequent effects upon the travel industry.

One of the difficulties in analysing cases is the lack of a *'right'* answer. Whilst there may be some answers that are clearly *'wrong'*, it is less easy to prove that an answer is right. If for instance you propose that a one-branch travel agency that has demonstrated growth of 10% per annum over the past five years should grow to become the largest travel agency group in the country over the next three years, it would almost certainly be unrealistic and therefore wrong. However, there may be several strategic options available and the strength of the answer depends upon the strength of the arguments presented, which in turn depend upon the analysis carried out. The analysis should be based upon the facts of the case, sound reasoning and importantly the application of strategic principles, theories and concepts from the academic literature.

Doing the Analysis

A few tips on the analysis of cases are presented below:

- *Read the case thoroughly* – Read the case twice initially. First read the case quickly as if you were reading a newspaper, getting a feel for the structure and layout of the case. On the second reading, make notes, underline important passages, mark sections for later analysis and identify the central issues. Once you have an adequate grasp of the case and the issues presented you can begin an in-depth analysis.

- *Organise the case facts* – The facts of a case may be presented in a bewildering or misleading way. It may be necessary for you to reorganise the information or label the data so that it makes more sense. For instance, sometimes it might be necessary to reorder the material chronologically or to separate the organisation into its constituent parts.
- *Avoid vacuous terms* – Terms that are hollow and lacking in content make the analysis unsound. For example, 'good', 'bad', 'many', 'few' are vacuous, as each individual could interpret them in a different manner. Instead use precise language.
- *Do not contact the company* – The case provides the information you need to analyse and the information may have been changed for teaching purposes. The case is designed to put you in the position of a company manager at a particular point in time. What actually happened is not relevant and companies should not be burdened by numerous student enquiries.
- *Appeals to authority* – Use of references, concepts and empirical evidence to support your case are valid ways of justifying your arguments. However, care must be taken. Just because an expert supports a view does not necessarily make it correct and different experts can present different views.
- *Apply concepts* – If you use a concept to organise the information or to support your views make sure that it is applied appropriately. For example, Porter's five forces model may be an appropriate way of analysing the competitive environment but make sure that it is applied to the facts of the case and not merely presented in its abstract form. A common mistake is to

use every conceivable strategic concept or framework available. Be selective, usually some concepts are more appropriate in the circumstances than others. The concepts are only useful inasmuch that they aid understanding. Which concepts are appropriate will depend upon the facts of the case and the material presented to you.

- *Look for linkages* – The case may be presented in a confusing manner but look for opportunities to make links between different parts of the case and thereby demonstrate that you have understood the case and its complexities. For instance, the case may state within the text that a new sales and marketing director was appointed. In another part of the case a table may indicate a falling sales trend and the financial statements may indicate a vastly increased advertising budget. By bringing together the three disparate pieces of information, appropriate conclusions might be drawn. Similarly, bringing together information from differing parts of the case and presenting it in a different form may be useful to aid understanding. For example, putting figures into a graph or table.
- *Look for ways of adding value to the information* – Look for opportunities when analysing a case to add value through your analysis. In other words, it is of far more value to interpret the information rather than merely to repeat the information contained in the case in your answer. For example, a case on an airline might state that the aircraft fleet contains 10 Boeing 737 – 400 and 6 Boeing 757 aircraft purchased at various stated dates between 1986 and 1997. Rather than repeat this information in your answer it is much more useful to calculate the average age of the fleet. Is the fleet relatively young or relatively old? Similarly a tour operator may present sales figures for the last ten years. A calculation showing the percentage growth (or decline) of sales from year to year would add value. Such a calculation would clearly show whether the rate of growth has risen or declined.

CASE 1
STRATEGIC ALLIANCES IN THE AIRLINE INDUSTRY

Introduction

The airline sector has a long history of working in partnerships. In 1999, 513 international alliances existed between airline companies, an increase of about 80% from the 1994 level. Under the auspices of the International Air Transport Association (IATA), a tradition of cooperation between airlines was built up and on individual routes cooperation has commonly included revenue-pooling agreements between the carriers operating a route.

During the 1990s, airlines have rushed to form alliances in the fear of being left behind and the stage has now been reached where the international airline sector is coalescing into a small number of large alliance groupings such as the *Star Alliance* which includes Lufthansa, United Airlines and Scandinavian Airlines System (SAS), the *Oneworld Alliance* which includes British Air ways, American Airlines and Qantas, and the longstanding alliance between KLM and Northwest Airlines. It is not only the number of airline alliance agreements being made that is significant, but the deepening relations between partners in these alliances. 'No longer are alliances mere loose arrangements between a couple of carriers to share flight codes and cross-sell tickets', the alliances are now so wide ranging that 'they are aiming at virtual mergers, despite national rules forbidding foreign ownership' (*The Economist*, 1998).

Motivations for Alliance Formation in the Airline Sector

British Airways attempted to introduce a degree of empiricism to the analysis of the external forces driving alliance formation. It used scenario-planning techniques to develop strategies for the future given the uncertainties in the macroenvironment. Scenarios representing possible futures were developed which sought to identify the key driving forces shaping the world economy and in turn the airline industry. Enormous changes have occurred in technology, education, world trade and finance over the past 50 years with a quickening pace of change. The combination of these forces has helped to bring about the information 'revolution', global economic restructuring and global competition.

External Drivers

The Information 'Revolution'

In the 1960s and 1970s information technologies mainly played a facilitating role in international tourism. The US Airline Deregulation Act of 1978 introduced airlines operating in the USA to a new world of competitive threats and opportunities. The key change, whereby price regulating power was removed from the Civil Aeronautics Board (CAB), enabled airlines to increase the variety of fares offered and the increased frequency by which fares were changed necessitated the extensive development of advanced Computer Reservations Systems (CRS). The CRS systems allowed airlines to monitor, manage and control their capacity through yield management and their clients through 'frequent flyer' programmes. The growth in CRS systems, first in the USA and then in Europe and elsewhere, created a marketing tool of considerable power, given travel agents' preferences for booking flights on their screens as the customer is waiting. In the past the airlines that owned the CRSs undoubtedly favoured their own flights (or those of their code sharing partners), but to a significant extent such bias has now been eliminated, at least in Europe and North America, through codes of conduct. The power given to airlines by the CRS system has now been replicated by the power given directly to consumers by the Internet. A vast amount of information is available to consumers to compare prices and the Internet's growth has allowed airlines to communicate directly with consumers thus cutting out the need for intermediaries to be involved. Some airlines such as easyJet are making extensive use of the technology, reporting that over 80% of bookings are being made through the Internet.

Economic Restructuring

Economic restructuring through the philosophy of 'economic disengagement' by governments in many parts of the world, has, since the 1970s, had a major impact on airline industry structure. This philosophy influenced by the widespread adoption of the theory of 'contestable markets' (which advocated the removal of restrictive industry entry barriers) from the early 1980s, manifested itself in the forms of deregulation and privatisation. The Chicago Convention of 1944 established the bilateral system of air service agreements (between pairs of national governments), which have since governed international air transport. The international industry that developed was characterised by national airlines from each country serving routes, airlines charging the same fares, and often sharing markets and revenues. Some bilateral agreements also involved agreement on such matters as ground handling. The terms of the bilateral agreements reflected the negotiating power and current aviation policies of the countries involved and resulting productivity was often low and costs were high.

Deregulation of domestic services occurred in the United States in 1978 followed by Canada, the United Kingdom, Australia and New Zealand in the 1980s, and the completion of deregulation within the European Union in April 1997. However, parallel liberalisation in international air services has taken place much more slowly. Notwithstanding the change that has occurred in some markets, even the liberalised structures are restrictive on industry entry. Requirements for designated airlines to be owned by nationals of the states involved are common and airport congestion and slot allocation practices often further impede effective industry entry. There was some evidence, however, that the removal of bilateral agreements and similar intervention barriers can reduce fares.

Another, and linked, aspect of economic disengagement is the worldwide movement towards the privatisation of state owned airlines. Despite this gradual process, however, many international airlines remain publicly owned or have major government shareholdings. Controls on foreign ownership remain in most national industries but some foreign ownership now exists, and with planned privatisations, this will increase.

The European Union's third air transport package (implemented from April 1997), for instance, sets no limit on the stake an EU national or EU airline can hold in an airline registered in another European Union state. With limited exceptions, however, non-European Union investors cannot hold a majority stake in any EU airline. In the USA, foreign shareholdings of up to 49% of equity under certain circumstances and 25% of voting stock is possible, although the US government also imposes an *ad hoc* control test to determine whether the foreign shareholder would substantially influence decision-making irrespective of equity held.

Liberalisation, privatisation, foreign ownership and transnational mergers will have a major impact upon the future structure of the airline industry but many regulatory and ownership barriers remain in force worldwide. As a result alternative methods of strategic development, namely internally generated growth, and mergers and acquisitions are often precluded as viable growth strategies for international airlines, and consequently the formation of strategic alliances is, in many cases, the only available form of new market entry.

Global Competition

Organisational 'type' has been dramatically influenced by the rise of globalisation and it has been argued that success or failure of larger businesses in the future will depend upon their ability to compete globally. Certainly many industries in the post-war era have seen a rapid concentration of activity with the emergence of a few dominant companies. Global competition is clearly well advanced in industries such as motor vehicles, pharmaceuticals, soft drinks and, more recently, financial services, but globalisation is a more recent phenomenon in the airline business, having been restricted for so long by regulation, government ownership and consumer preferences.

Airlines are seeking to maximise their 'global reach', in the belief that those that offer a global service (with a competitively credible presence in each of the major air travel markets) will be in the strongest competitive position. In a global airline context, the triad is modified so as to broaden the Japanese leg of the triad to include the wider Asia-Pacific region and for the crucial markets to include not only the constitutent markets of the triad but also the flows between them. Thus, globalisation, and particularly developments in the key markets, is an important external driver for alliance formation.

Internal Drivers

Risk Sharing

Strategic alliances are seen as an attractive mechanism for hedging risk because neither partner bears the full risk and cost of the alliance activity. The need to spread the costs and risk of innovation has increased as capital requirements for development projects have risen. Developing new or existing routes, for instance, becomes far less risky if the partners operating the routes have firmly entrenched marketing strengths in the two markets at either end of the routes.

Economies of Scale, Scope and Learning

A prime driver for alliance formation is for airlines to achieve cost economies, which can be categorised as economies of scale, scope and experience. Economies of scale exist where the average cost per unit of output declines as the level of output increases. Empirical evidence reveals little evidence of economies of scale, however, except for the smallest operators and in specific areas such as marketing. Indeed one study of US domestic aviation suggests possible diseconomies at the largest airlines. Furthermore, the evidence also suggests that airlines' unit costs do not fall greatly as they expand their networks. Cost savings stem from attracting more traffic to a given network rather than expanding it to cover more destinations.

The airline industry may lack substantial scale economies, but other economies related to the size and nature of operations exist which help to explain the growing industry concentration and the move towards alliances. Economies of scope occur when the cost of producing two (or more) products jointly is less than the cost of producing each one alone. Such economies can be achieved if alliance partners link up their existing, networks so that they can provide connecting services for new markets, and where marketing costs can be shared between alliance partners.

For example, the alliance between KLM and Northwest formed in 1989 has had a substantial impact on passenger numbers, market share and both airlines' financial performance. Through the alliance, KLM has gained access to Northwest's extensive North American route network based on its Minneapolis, Detroit and Boston hubs, whilst Northwest can advertise that it serves KLM's sizeable international network.

A number of observers have suggested that an important motivator in forming alliances is the benefit to be derived from economies of learning (or experience). Incumbent suppliers have more information on the market being served and can tailor their services to specific customer needs. Whereas new entrants would have to sink resources to acquire such information in order to win market share, alliances allow the information to be gained from existing suppliers.

Access to Assets, Resources and Competences

Specific resource, skill or competence inadequacy can be addressed by collaborating with partners which have a different set of such attributes and can therefore compensate for internal deficiencies. The regulatory framework of 'bilaterals' and landing rights means that slots at congested airports are important and marketable assets that are attractive to alliance partners. Alliances can thus offer relatively easy access to a route through allowing access to a partner's assets which may have been established over prolonged periods and which may have been previously protected by government intervention.

Shape Competition

Strategic alliances can influence the companies that a firm competes with and the basis of competition. They can also reduce the likelihood of retaliatory behaviour by binding two firms together as allies. Furthermore, current strategic positions may be successfully defended against forces that are too strong for one firm to withstand alone. Strategic alliances may, therefore, be used as a defensive ploy to reduce competition since an obvious benefit of strategic alliances is converting a competitor into a partner. Smaller and weaker airlines may view alliances as the only viable way in which to compete with larger, more sophisticated rivals. The announcement in March 1998 by Air Lanka that it was to sell a 40% stake to Emirates Airlines, for instance, was viewed as part of a defensive alliance strategy aimed at retaining international competitiveness through allying with a commercially stronger rival.

Alternatively, alliance formation may form part of an offensive strategy. By linking with a rival pressure can be put on the profits and market share of a common competitor. The proposed alliance between British Airways and American Airlines announced in June 1996 was seen as such a case since it represented the combining of (arguably) the two strongest airlines on the transatlantic routes. It therefore attracted widespread criticism from competing airlines and later failed to win regulatory approval from either the US or EU authorities.

Alliance Structure and Scope

Considerable time and effort may be expended in developing the structure and scope of an alliance. The unique nature and operating environment of the airline sector means that alliances must be structured around diverse requirements. Determining the structure and scope of an alliance requires detailed consideration of issues across a broad spectrum.

Issues that must be taken into account include marketing, products, computer system technologies, equipment and equipment servicing and logistics.

Evaluation of Alliance Performance

Evaluating the performance of alliances is complex given the multifaceted objectives of many alliances and the difficulties involved in ascribing financial measures. The situation is often further complicated by the asymmetric performance: one firm achieves its objectives while others fail to do so. For instance, several alliances have resulted in a situation where one partner raced to learn the other's skills while the other partner had no such intentions.

Despite these evident measurement obstacles, several observers have attempted empirical studies of alliance performance, primarily through examining the factors leading to the termination of alliance arrangements. These contributory factors include partner asymmetry, competitive overlap between partners, the presence of other concurrent ties, and the characteristics of the alliance itself, such as autonomy of operations of flexibility. It should be borne in mind, however, that not all alliance terminations can be viewed as failures since in some cases they may have been intended as time-limited arrangements. Furthermore, it should not be assumed that all continuing alliances are successful since intertia or high exit costs may provide an explanation for their continuation.

Examples of Airline Alliance Success and Failure

The 'Alcazar' alliance involving Scandinavian Airline System (SAS), Swissair, Austrian Airlines and KLM failed in the early 1990s partly because the individual airlines were technologically incompatible (they used different CRS systems). In another example, British Airways held discussions at various times with KLM, Sabena and United Airlines regarding strategic alliances before forming such an alliance with US Airways in July 1992 as part of its strategy of building up several key global collaborative agreements.

The agreement between British Airways and US Airways (which involved the acquisition of approximately 44% of US Airways' equity share capital by British Airways), has now been broken, with British Airways writing off 50% of its initial investment. The British Airways/US Airways alliance provides an example of poor long-term positioning in that the alliance stood in the way of more recent strategies by both partners. In June 1996, British Airways announced its intention to form a wider alliance with American Airlines (which still awaits regulatory approval as at year 2002), and US Airways responded with a lawsuit seeking damages. US Airways is said to have been anxious to extricate itself from its alliance with British Airways because it failed to deliver the projected earnings enhancement. British Airways, on the other hand, viewed American Airlines as a larger strategically, more important alliance partner. The long list of failed airline alliances, supposedly bolstered by equity stakes, includes Air Canada/Continental Airlines, Scandinavian Airlines System/ Continental Airlines and Sabena Air France.

Political sensitivities lay behind the failure of another proposed airline alliance between the Dutch airline KLM and Belgian airline Sabena in the early 1990s. Both airlines had held talks with British Airways before talking to each other about a possible alliance or merger. Both were loss-making and feared absorption by larger competitors, but the failure to cement an alliance highlighted the uniquely political nature of the airline sector. Political considerations are transparent when both companies involved are 'national flag carriers' carrying the prestige of the home country around the world. For Sabena to ally with KLM would have created a predominantly Dutch-speaking company which would have proved politically unacceptable in bilingual Belgium. Sabena had to bow to political pressure from Belgium's French-speaking community and pull out of negotiations.

The airline alliance between KLM and the American airline Northwest dating from 1989 can claim to be a success, at least in part, since it has shown uncharacteristic sustainability, and appears to have been revenue-enhancing for the two partners. The alliance, which encompasses collaboration on a broad front including code-sharing, flight scheduling, joint marketing, and integration of frequent flyer programmes, had generated additional revenues of between $125 million and $175 million for Northwest and $100 million for KLM by 1994. Through the alliance KLM gained access to Northwest's extensive North American route network based on its Minneapolis, Detroit and Boston hubs, whilst Northwest can advertise that it serves KLM's sizeable international network through its Amsterdam hub.

The alliance was borne out of necessity when KLM, (in return for a 20% equity stake), contributed $400 million to the $700 million that was required when senior Northwest executives put together a leveraged buyout of the airline. Notwithstanding the financial success of this strategic alliance, cultural differences and personal incompatibilities between the two parties have repeatedly threatened to force them apart and have at times soured the relationship. One writer noted that, 'the alliance has been a saga of personal spats, fights over "creeping control" and threats of separation that until recently were hidden behind a marriage that works well on a daily basis'. KLM, it is said, is inclined to be quiet, stay out of the limelight and focus on strong operational expertise whereas the US partner (Northwest) is more inclined to Hollywood lifestyles and a financial engineering approach to management.

Appendix 6.1.1
Airline Alliances in the Global Airline Industry, 1994 – 1999

	1994	*1995*	*1996*	*1997*	*1998*	*1999*	*% Change 99/94*
Number of alliances	280	324	389	363	502	513	+183%
with equity stakes	58	58	62	54	56	53	–8.6%
non-equity alliances	222	266	327	309	446	460	+207.2%
New alliances	–	50	71	72	121	26	
Number of airlines	136	153	159	177	196	204	+150.0%

Source: Adapted from Airline Business, 1999.

Appendix 6.1.2
Major International Airline Alliances as at July 1999

Alliance members	*Date joined*	*Passenger traffic 1998 (RPK bn)*	*Passenger traffic 1998 world share*	*Passenger numbers millions*	*Revenue $ billons*
		Atlantic Excellence/Qualifier			
Atlantic Excellence					
Austrian Airlines	Jun 96	7.3	0.3%	3.4	1.3
Delta Air Lines	Jun 96	166.3	6.3%	105.4	14.4
Sabena	Jun 96	15.3	0.6%	8.7	2.4
Swissair	Jun 96	28.0	1.1%	11.9	7.8
Sub totals		***216.9***	***8.2%***	***129.5***	***25.9***
Qualifier					
Air Europe	May 99	5.8	0.2%	0.8	0.2
AOM	Mar 98	8.5	0.3%	2.9	0.6
Austrian Airlines	Mar 98	7.3	0.3%	3.4	1.3
Crossair	Mar 98	2.7	0.1%	4.4	N/a
Lauda Air	Mar 98	2.9	0.1%	0.8	N/a
Sabena	Mar 98	15.3	0.6%	8.7	2.4
Swissair	Mar 98	28.0	1.1%	11.9	7.8
TAP Air Portugal	Mar 98	9.4	0.4%	4.5	0.9
THY Turkish Airlines	Mar 98	13.0	0.5%	9.9	1.4
Sub totals		***93.0***	***3.5%***	***47.4***	***14.6***
Total		*259.3*	*9.9%*	*152.8*	*29.0*
		Oneworld			
American Airlines	Sep 98	175.2	6.7%	81.4	19.2
British Airways	Sep 98	116.0	4.4%	36.6	14.6
Canadian	Sep 98	26.9	1.0%	8.3	2.1
Cathay Pacific	Sep 98	40.7	1.5%	10.3	3.4
Qantas	Sep 98	56.9	2.2%	16.4	5.2
Sub totals		***415.7***	***15.8%***	***153.0***	***30.0***
Future members					
Flinair		10.2	0.4%	6.8	1.5
Iberia		32.5	1.2%	21.8	3.6
Lan Chile		8.7	0.3%	4.0	1.1
Total		***467.1***	***17.8%***	***185.5***	***36.2***
		Star Alliance			
Air Canada	May 97	37.3	1.4%	15.0	4.0
Lufthansa	May 97	75.4	2.9%	38.5	12.8
SAS	May 97	20.8	0.8%	21.5	5.2

Alliance members	*Date joined*	*Passenger traffic 1998 (RPK bn)*	*Passenger traffic 1998 world share*	*Passenger numbers millions*	*Revenue $ billons*
Thai International	May 97	34.4	1.3%	15.6	2.5
United Airlines	May 97	200.4	7.6%	88.6	17.6
Varig	Oct 97	27.1	1.0%	11.0	3.0
Ansett Australia	Mar 99	13.1	0.5%	11.7	2.0
Air New Zealand	Mar 99	19.4	0.7%	6.2	1.7
Sub totals		***428.0***	***16.3%***	***206.3***	***48.8***
Future members					
All Nippon Airways		54.4	2.1%	42.3	7.1
Singapore Airlines		58.2	2.2%	12.4	2.7
Total		***540.6***	***20.6%***	***261.0***	***58.6***
		Northwest/KLM			
Alitalia	May 99	35.6	1.4%	24.2	5.0
Continental	Jan 99	86.7	3.3%	43.6	8.0
KLM	1989	57.3	2.2%	15.0	22.0
Northwest Airlines	1989	107.4	4.1%	50.5	9.0
Total		***287.0***	***10.9%***	***133.3***	***44.0***

RPK, Revenue Passenger Kilometres.
Source: Adapted from Airline Business (1999).

Appendix 6.1.3
External Driving Forces Underpinning Strategic Alliance Formation in the Airline Industry

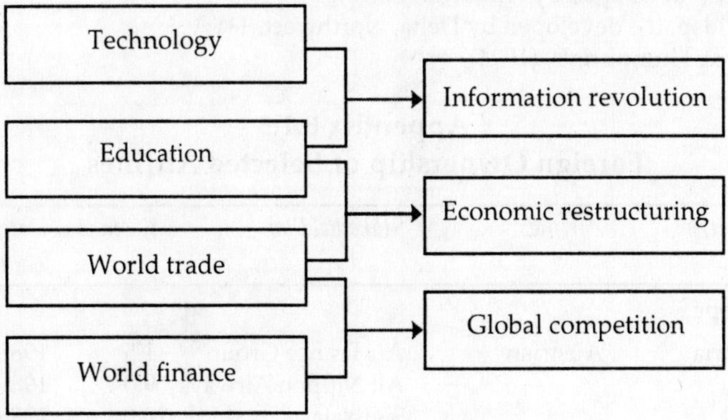

Source: Moyer (1996).

Appendix 6.1.4
CRS Market Share in European Countries

Country	*Amadeus (% of locations)*	*Galileo (% of locations)*	*Sabre (%of locations)*	*Worldspan (% of locations)*
Austria	34.8	60.4	3.1	1.6
Belgium	21.1	30.1	16.0	32.8
Denmark	54.2	14.1	6.9	24.8
Finland	98.1	–	1.7	0.2
France	81.7	4.1	10.1	4.1
Germany	91.6	1.4	4.7	2.3
Greece	–	39.9	34.9	25.2
Hungary	–	97.6	2.4	–
Ireland	–	84.6	6.0	9.4
Italy	–	76.9	17.8	5.3
Luxembourg	57.1	–	42.9	–
Netherlands	–	61.6	10.3	26.8
Norway	74.5	11.2	7.7	6.6
Portugal	6.0	65.5	0.2	28.3
Spain	88.7	5.2	2.6	3.5
Sweden	77.0	–	13.0	10.0
Switzerland	–	87.7	9.9	2.4
UK	0.2	65.6	20.0	14.2

Notes:

Amadeus – developed by Air France, Lufthansa, Iberia, Sabena.

Galileo – developed by British Airways, KLM, Swissair, Austrian, Aer Lingus, Air Portugal, Olympic.

Sabre – developed by American Airlines.

Worldspan – developed by Delta, Northwest, TWA.

Source: Humphreys, (1994).

Appendix 6.1.5
Foreign Ownership of Selected Airlines

Country	*Airline*	*Stake held by*	*% stake*	*Date first acquired*
Europe				
Austria	Austrian	Air France Group	1.5	1988
		All Nippon Airways	9.0	1989
		Swissair	10.0	1988
	Lauda Air	Austrian	35.9	1996
		Lufthansa	20.0	1993

Country	*Airline*	*Stake held by*	*% stake*	*Date first acquired*
Belgium	Sabena	Swissair	49.5	1995
France	Air Liberte	British Airways	70	1992
Germany	Deutsche BA	British Airways	100	1992
Luxembourg	Luxair	Lufthansa	13.0	1992
Spain	Spanair	SAS	49.0	1986
Switzerland	Swissair	Delta Air Lines	4.5	1989
		Singapore Airlines	2.7	1991
Ukraine	Ukraine Int'l Airlines	Austrian Airlines	14.3	1996
		Swissair	4.1	1996
United Kingdom	British Midland	SAS	40.0	1988
North America				
USA	Delta Airlines	Singapore Airlines	3	1991
		Swissair	3	1989
Canada	Canadian Airlines	American Airlines	33.0	1994
Asia/Pacific				
Australia	Ansett Australia	Air New Zealand	50.0	1996
	Qantas	British Airways	25.0	1993
China	Dragonair	Cathay Pacific	25.5	1990
Malaysia	Malaysia Airlines	Royal Brunei	10.0	Not reported
Singapore	Singapore Airlines	Delta Air Lines	2.7	1991
		Swissair	0.6	1991
Other				
Argentina	Aerolinas Argentinas	Iberia Airlines	10.0	1990
		American Airlines	10.0	1997
Mauritius	Air Mauritius	Air France	12.8	1975
		Air India	8.8	1975
		British Airways	12.8	1975
Kenya	Kenya Airways	KLM	26.0	1995

Source: Adapted from *Airline Business* (1999).

Appendix 6.1.6
Share of World RPKs* and World RPK Growth

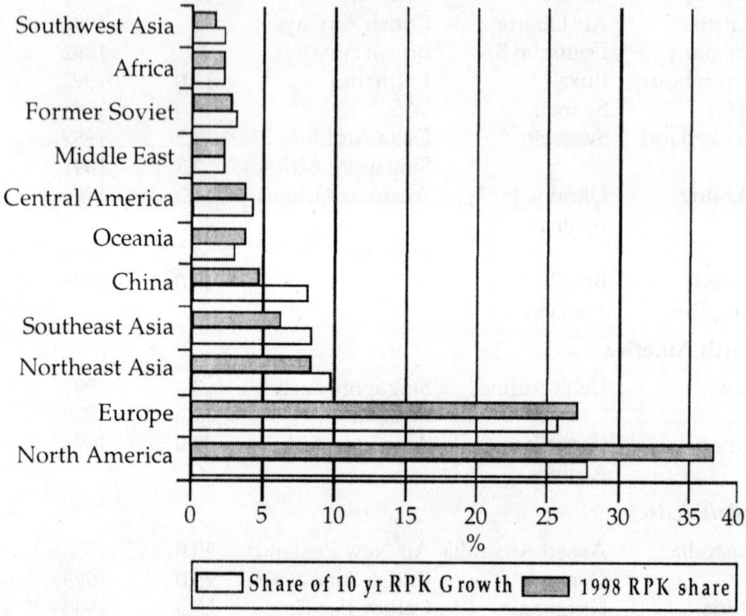

*RPK, Revenue Passenger Kilometres.
Source: Adapted from Boeing (1999).

Sources

Airlines Business (1999) Circling the Globe – Annual Alliances Survey, *Airline Business*, July, 33 – 65.

Boeing Aircraft Company (1999) *Current Market Outlook – Economic Basis of Traffic Growth*, http:/www.boeing.com/commercial/cmo/3eb06.html regional.

The Economist (1998) Airline Alliances: Mergers in Mind, *The Economist*, 26 September, p. 96.

Humphreys, B.K. (1994) The Implications of International Code Sharing, *Journal of Air Transport Management*, 1(4), 195 – 207.

CASE 2
HOLIDAYBREAK PLC: ADAPTING FOR SUCCESS

Origins and Development

Holidaybreak plc is, together with MyTravel plc and First Choice plc, one of only three quoted tour operators currently trading on the London Stock Exchange. Although considerably smaller than the other two, Holidaybreak plc evolved from the Eurocamp camping business and is a specialised travel business of significant scale. It operates on a pan-European basis.

The camping holiday market has seen many developments over the past 30 years or so. Camping was viewed as an activity merely for scouts and the adventurous, and was associated in the public mind with leaking canvas tents lacking adequate ground sheets. There was clearly a gap in the market – to provide camping holidays that would appeal to the wider public. The first company to exploit this gap with self drive camping holidays was Canvas Holidays, which was established in 1965 by Jack Cuthbert. The company's first site was in Brittany, France, utilising traditional tents, but gradually the product evolved to provide the luxury tents which later became associated with camping at destinations in numerous European countries.

The year 1973 marked the founding of Eurocamp with the provision of self-drive camping holidays to a single French camp site, offered to British customers through direct sales. The company enjoyed a decade of growth under its founder Alan Goulding, culminating in the sale of the company to Combined English Stores plc (CES) in 1983. At this time the company's capacity had grown to over 50 camp sites, mainly in France but also in Switzerland, Germany and Italy. Mobile home holidays were also added in that year.

By the mid-1980s, Eurocamp had established itself as the market leader in the provision of self-drive camping holidays to continental Europe from the UK. In 1984 the offering of Eurocamp holidays to the Dutch market through a sales agent was initiated and some holidays were sold in the UK through agents. Two smaller direct sell camping operators were acquired by CES in 1986: Carefree Camping Ltd. and Sunsites Ltd. Eurocamp Independent was launched in 1987 providing holidays for customers using their own tents.

Next Plc, a leading fashion retailer (which had been expanding rapidly in the early 1980s), bought CES in 1987 and it later became apparent that it was seeking potential purchasers for some of its non-core activities in order to reduce its high levels of debt. Richard Atkinson, Holidaybreak's chief executive, explained that, 'Next was unloading its peripherals, the classic scenario for a management buyout. We wanted independence and there was a significant financial incentive.'

Management and Organisation

Richard Atkinson had spotted his chance. He had begun his career in classic travel industry fashion as a courier, being Eurocamp's first full-time employee in 1976 after graduating from Manchester University. Good career moves often occur by accident, and his move stemmed from nothing more than, 'a vague desire to work in France'. Atkinson turned down a job offer from Canvas Holidays, the market leaders from the early 1970s.

Eurocamp was lucky with the timing of its entry to the market because in a niche market that was in its infancy, the company was able to learn from established competitors. As one of the first companies to compete with Canvas, Eurocamp had the opportunity to learn from Canvas and avoid the mistakes that had previously been made in the fledgling sector. Atkinson grew with the company, taking responsibility for operations and marketing before becoming general manager in 1979, when he took over day-to-day running of the company. Following the resignation of the founder in 1983, he became managing director.

Atkinson recalled, 'by 1981 we were number two in the market. There were a lot of companies trying to do the same thing, but we had looked at what Canvas Holidays did and tried to do it better, rather than just accepting we were second fiddle, and we overtook them a few years later.' Recession hit the travel trade in the early 1980s and the number of companies involved in the camping holiday market contracted sharply with Eurocamp strengthening its position as a result in a market that continued to exhibit growth.

Two of Eurocamp's original executive board members, Martin Leppard (operations) and Julian Rawel (sales and marketing), both followed similar routes into the company. The fourth member of the management team, Gordon Harman, a chartered accountant (who became finance director in 1984 after joining the company in 1982), brought with him much needed financial expertise. The management team was strengthened by the appointment of Jim Crew (group systems) in 1989 after five years' involvement with the company on a consultancy basis. The group also had non-executive involvement at board level. Tom Neville was appointed non-executive chairman in July 1990 having previously retired as the finance director of Vickers plc, a major defence company. Gil Thompson, the chief executive of Manchester Airport was appointed to the board in March 1991.

In the early days the group was very much dominated by the forcefulness of its founder. The chairman based decisions very much on instinct and rarely were these decisions challenged. As the company grew, and when the founder left the company, the company's management began to evolve in different ways. A group of senior managers developed, taking decisions together after consideration of the issues, while management expertise of a more technical nature was bought in as required. Although senior managers took increasingly specialised roles within the group and a well-defined reporting structure existed, members of the management team took an active interest informally in other areas of the business in order to maintain an overall perspective.

In November 1988 a management buy-out was led by the management team and Eurocamp plc was formed. 'We had great deal of experience of the way the business was growing,' said Atkinson, who believed this to be an important prerequisite for any management buy-out. 'When everyone knows each other and the team is experienced, there can be continuity of business, despite changes in company ownership.' A number of institutional investors; led by Barelays Development Capital Ltd., backed the buy-out in the form of loans and equity totalling £32 million.

After the management buy-out the group continued to expand and develop and was floated as Eurocamp plc on the London Stock Exchange in 1991. Several directors later left the company and other directors joined the main board as businesses were added. The group, which became more diverse and complex, was organised into three divisions (Camping, Hotel Breaks and Adventure), each of which was represented at main board of director level. In recent years Holidaybreak has sought to operate quality, market-leading businesses in sectors of the holiday business which appear to offer good growth potential. The low-margin, short-haul air-inclusive tour package holiday market has been avoided, thereby choosing not to compete head-to-head with the large vertically integrated tour operators.

The board of directors has overall responsibility for ensuring that the company maintains a system of internal financial control to provide them with reasonable assurance regarding the reliability of financial information used within the business and that assets are safeguarded. Subsidiary businesses produce monthly management accounts information which is used to compare actual performance with budget and medium term plans. These accounts include updated forecasts and other information to enable the board to assess the prospects of all group businesses. The group has an established internal organisational structure with clear well defined reporting lines, which determine responsibilities and areas of accountability.

The group maintains offices in various locations to manage the individual businesses. However, certain of the group's key functions, including the company secretariat, legal, taxation, cash and currency management (treasury) and business risk insurance, are carried out centrally under the direct control of the group chief executive and the group finance director. The board has applied Principle D2 of the 'combined code' on corporate governance, which was published by the London Stock Exchange in 1998. The principle establishes a continuous process for identifying, evaluating and managing the significant risks that the group faces. Furthermore, the process itself is regularly reviewed. Such a system is designed to manage rather than to eliminate the risk of failure to achieve business objectives, and can only provide reasonable not absolute assurance against losses or misstatements in the accounts.

Activities and Operations – Camping

The principal activity of the group remains the provision of self-drive camping holidays in Europe, which are provided by the Camping division. This includes the hiring out of 'luxury' fully equipped tents and mobile homes at an extensive range of high standard European camp sites. The choice of holiday destinations amounts to over 250 in France and many other countries. The standard of accommodation provided is far removed from the traditional camping image. This is reflected in the standard of quality of the tents, mobile homes and camp sites provided. The majority of sites are included in their country's top official category (four star in France).

It is an important feature of the holidays that the character and ambience of the camp sites is preserved. In order to facilitate this aim, it is unusual for the group to rent more than 30% of the pitches on any one site. Furthermore, contracted pitches are usually spread throughout a site Holidays offered by the group differ from the standardised 'typical package' in a number of important respects. Holidays are not for standardised periods or at just one destination. Customers are offered freedom, flexibility and independence through a 'tailor made' combination, normally including cross-channel ferries of the customer's choice, insurance and accommodation. Motorail, fly/drive and en-route stops can also be added. On site the group have trained couriers.

The price of holidays offered cover a broad spectrum from but an important thrust of Eurocamp marketing at all price points is to be perceived as offering value for money. Well-established relationships have been developed with a large number of individual camp site owners. The highest number of pitches for tents and mobile homes rented from any one owner represents less than 5% of total group capacity. Ferry bookings are made with a number of different operators, principally Stena-Sealink, P&O, and Brittany Ferries. On-site operations are overseen by a team of experienced area managers. These managers supervise, train and support seasonal courier staff and monitor the quality of the product. They are also responsible for setting up and clearing the camp sites at the end of the season. On-site seasonal staff are employed mainly as couriers usually on full or half season contracts. In the past seasonal employees have been important sources of recruitment for permanent posts. Typically the group's products, in both the UK and overseas, are aimed at the family holiday market, with parents in the 30 – 45 age range from the ABC1 social categories. The holidays are also popular with couples, particularly at inland destinations outside the school holiday period. The majority of customers book direct although the Keycamp brand also receives a significant number of UK bookings through travel agents. A high level of customer satisfaction is achieved and a considerable amount of customers represent repeat bookings.

The group is the largest provider of self-drive camping holidays in Europe. The UK market is served by a small number of fairly long-established specialist operators but during recent years there has also been increased competition from other tour operators diversifying into this sector. The number of competitors in this sector of the market has increased markedly over recent years with about 100 companies currently competing in it. Traditionally, the sector has been dominated by specialists that have grown with the growth of the sector. These companies include Canvas Holidays, which is a well-established family owned concern, and French Life, a relatively small family-controlled business. Increasingly though, larger tour operators and companies with parent companies outside the travel industry have been attracted to the sector. These competitors included:

- Keycamp, which was owned by a diversified plc before its purchase by Holidaybreak.
- Haven, owned by Bourne Leisure (a privately owned company which also runs UK caravan parks and owns Butlins Holiday Centres).
- Eurosites, owned by MyTravel plc, which entered the market in the early 1990s.

Like its parent company, Eurosites is strongly price conscious, and sells its products both through the trade and 'direct sell'. The company has rapidly built up market share in this sector. Eurosites has a very fresh image. The identity is strong, easily remembered and used consistently throughout the company. The company's colours (blue and red), logo and brochure layout with widespread use of a white background all serve to establish its strong public image.

Holidaybreak has a number of brands. The *Eurocamp* brand (which together with the *Sunsites* and *Eurocamp Independent* brands is run from the company's Cheshire Head Office) is a direct sell business, aimed very much at the ABC1 markets. It is the clear market leader. The company has established a strong market identity using the company logo and the company colours (red and green) extensively. The Eurocamp brand competes directly with the well-established Canvas Holiday's product, which enjoys a loyal clientele. Canvas promotes its independence, its record and its informality.

Sunsites is a more simplified product based around the sun, sea, sand formula of Mediterranean holidays and is aimed particularly at families with small children. It is relatively easy for the trade to sell on a commission basis and is positioned slightly down-market of the Eurocamp brand.

The *Eurocamp Independent* brand allows people to take their own tents with them instead of using the company's contracted equipment. The company's role is to take care of the troublesome details, such as reservations, ferry bookings and insurance.

The *Keycamp* brand, which is managed from the brand's offices in Sutton, South-west London, has a strong following among travel agents as well as receiving many bookings through direct selling. The brand also has a far higher proportion than the Eurocamp brand of customers opting for mobile homes rather than camping.

The group has to compete in the wider market for overseas summer holidays. This involves competing with mainstream package holiday operators as well as other companies offering self-drive and self-catering family holidays in continental Europe. The self-drive sector represents only a small part of the total market, but in spite of the general trend away from the traditional package, it is believed that this sector will continue to grow.

Whilst it offers a cheaper alternative to air inclusive holidays, the quality of the product, wider choice of destinations and the willingness of the British to increasingly make their own way abroad, has produced a strong sector of the industry in its own right. Competition comes not so much from the Spanish Costas, but the country cottage market. The group has actively developed its holiday products so as to make them appeal to a wider customer base. Improvements in the level of comfort and quality of facilities have been made and the diversity and choice of destinations offered has been increased. The same high quality accommodation is available at all locations, but the nature of the holiday varies according to the style and environment of the camp site, the range and type of facilities and the approach of the site management.

The majority of bookings received by the group are secured through direct marketing and sales techniques, which offer a number of significant advantages. Additionally in recent years a number of new markets have been successfully developed. The group endeavours to manage its costs and capacity in a flexible way so as to match effective demand with supply as completely as operationally possible. Group companies rent space on selected camp sites usually on a seasonal basis. Unlike many other holiday companies, the group does not have a high level of committed costs, because there is not the requirement to charter aircraft seats for instance. Typically a contract gives considerable ability for the group to adjust the number of pitches rented. A substantial proportion of bookings is received prior to the turn of the calendar year and expenditure on camping equipment can be managed flexibly in accordance with requirements.

In contrast to most other package operators, therefore the business is more predictable, and phenomena such as 'consolidations', which see customers sent to a different location than the one originally booked, rarely happen. Holidaybreak is, however, susceptible to various problems of transportation arrangements caused by factors usually beyond the company's control such as problems with ferry operators or the operations of the Channel Tunnel.

One of Holidaybreak's main capital expenditure items is mobile homes. A popular form of holiday, the company has kept to strict limits on the proportion of capacity which such holidays represent, because of the need to retain flexibility in matching demand and supply. Cancellation rates are relatively high at about 10 – 12% of early bookings and perhaps 6% overall. Increasingly, the group has been able to spread demand across a number of months rather than being limited to the UK school summer holiday, resulting in high capacity utilisation throughout the season. Ferry crossings and insurance are not subject to fixed quotas, but are arranged as required. A large number of staff are employed on a seasonal basis only. The group thus has considerable flexibility in varying its major fixed and operating expenses in line with demand and thereby reducing the risk of late discounting of holiday prices. As a result the group is able to operate at far higher margins than have normally been associated with overseas tour operators.

Camping is the most mature of Holidaybreak's businesses, but several developments are taking place in this sector of the industry. Although the UK market is now fairly well served by well-established operators and is growing quite slowly, Holidaybreak has much lower levels of penetration in several European markets. Germany and mainland European markets are viewed as relatively under-exploited. There has also been a discernible move away from camping and towards mobile homes which offer greater degrees of comfort for customers. Mobile homes provide higher sales revenue at substantially higher margins.

Hotel Breaks

The group's second business is represented by its Hotel Breaks division, with which it has been involved since 1995. The business has agreements with about 1400 UK hotels which provide allocations to enable Hotel Break's brands, which include the market leading Superbreaks, to sell UK hotel short breaks normally for leisure customers and particularly at weekends. The company takes a 30% margin on the selling price, and a guarantee is provided to customers that they would not be able to book more cheaply by going directly to the hotel.

Although travel agents have hitherto provided the main distribution channel, direct sales and the Internet are growing in importance. There is a clear trend in the market for people to be taking more frequent short holidays, and weekend breaks are very much the current fashion.

Adventure

The Adventure division is the group's third business area and is the field in which the company has been most active in terms of acquisitions over recent years. A growing number of people demand more adventurous and exotic holidays as alternatives to lying on the beach or by a swimming pool. These customers, which come from a wide spectrum of age ranges, whilst wanting something a bit different, nevertheless want to feel secure in the quality of arrangements that are made. Explore Worldwide, which is based in Aldershot in Hampshire, is the UK market leader and the largest European operator of worldwide adventure holidays, with an estimated 40% of the UK market. Explore offers some 200 winter and summer tours to nearly 100 countries. An experienced tour leader leads each tour group comprising up to 18 people and customers will usually stay in middle range hotel accommodation, although some tours necessitate the use of more basic accommodation or camping.

The second business in this division is the much smaller Regal Diving, which is based in Cambridge. Regal travels mainly to the Red Sea organising scuba diving holidays and are the leading specialist operator in this particular market niche.

Financial Information

The Holidaybreak group has had a successful record of growth over the past five years, with an increasing number of sales being made in continental Europe. In addition, it has been possible to apply consistent pricing policies, thereby avoiding significant recourse to discounting. The group's business is of a highly seasonal nature, resulting in unbalanced profitability through the year and cyclical cash flows. However, in a typical year the group is net cash generative, with capital expenditure incurred at the beginning of the calendar year and normally significant cash balances being held by year end. During the winter months the group faces a negative cash position financed by bank overdrafts, with the peak overdraft requirement falling in January or February. Net cash flows into the group from February onwards, so that positive cash balances are held by the group for the remainder of the year. These balances peak in June or July.

The management of the cash flow of the group ('cash management') is thus a significant part of running the business. It is important to be able to forecast the size and timing of the major inflows and outflows of cash and the resulting cash balances or deficits that may result. With this information overdraft requirements can be planned for, negotiated and agreed with the bank. Additionally, interest income on cash balances represents highly significant source of revenue for the group.

As part of the cash management process, consideration is given to the nature of the booking terms, asking for payments from customers slightly earlier than the norm in order to improve cash flow. Inducements for early payment and rewards for returning customers in the form of discounts are given in some cases. The group's business is thus of a highly seasonal nature, with sales and profits being recognised in the second half of the year as holidays are taken. Intensive marketing of the following season's camping holidays commences in October each year, with the majority of bookings taken by April of the following year.

There remain accounting oddities inherent in Holidaybreak's business, not least because it has only limited fixed assets, with the value of the business resting largely in the goodwill associated with the brand names and the management expertise in place. Even so, the company has more fixed assets than many travel companies, with net book value camping equipment (mainly tents and mobile homes) representing substantial assets.

Currency exposure is always a topic of interest to companies offering overseas holidays. The company's net currency exposure is, however, very limited. Since there is also a substantial inflow of Euros from the foreign selling operations in Holland, Germany and to a lesser extent Ireland and other countries, a 'nature hedge' is provided against the principal expenses which are incurred in France (predominantly) and other countries. Any remaining net exposure to the risk of movements in currency rates is managed through the taking out of forward foreign exchange contacts with major banks.

Appendix 6.2.1
Holidaybreak plc Organisation chart – 2002

Holidaybreak plc – Board of Directors

Angus Crichton-Miller	Chairman (Formerly Chairman of Bank plc Leisure and Holiday Businesses)
Clive McLintock	Non-Executive Director (Formerly a Director of Barclays Bank Development Capital)
Peter Folkman	Non-Executive Director (Formerly as senior Banker based in Manchester)
Richard Atkinson	Chief Executive
Robert Baddeley	Finance Director
Simon Tobin	Managing Director Adverture Holidays Division
Jim Crew	Managing Director Camping Division
Mark Wray	Joint M.D. Superbreak
Nick Cust	Joint M.D. Superbreak
Julie Vickers	Company Secretary

Advanture Holidays Division

Simon Tomm (joined 1995)	Managing Director
Bill Mcwarm	Commercial Director, Explore
Derek Maure	Operations Director, Explore
Jo Field	Marketing Director, Explore

Camping Division

Jim Crew (joined 1989)	Managing Director
Steven Whitfield	Operations Director
Monwenna Angove	Sales & Marketing Dir. Eurocamp UK
Kay-Uwe Hermann	M.D. Eurocamp Germany
Dick Pootinga	M.D. Eurocamp Holland
Peter Franken	Development Director Eurocamp Holland
John Baines	M.D. Keycamp

Hotel Breaks Division

Mark Wray (joined 1995)	Joint M.D. Superbreak
Nick Cust (joined 1995)	Joint M.D. Superbreak
Frank Regan	Operations Director
Ian Mounser	Sales Director
Ray Jones	Brand Development Manager

Note: Richard Atkinson and Robert Baddeley also sit as non-executive members on the board of directors of each operating division.

Appendix 6.2.2
A Brief History of Holidaybreak plc

Holidaybreak plc was founded in 1973 as Eurocamp Travel Limited – a family-run business, based in Knutsford, Cheshire, offering camping holidays in Brittany. From modest beginnings the business grew steadily benefiting from the growing interest in France as a holiday business. In the early 1980s mobile-homes and destinations outside France were added to the product range. Ownership of the business changed in 1981, with the founder Alan Goulding selling to the London based retail group Combined English Stores plc. Alan Goulding finally left the company in 1983 when Richard Atkinson, currently chief executive, became managing director.

The 1980s were years of innovation and growth as the UK market to France expanded rapidly and Eurocamp took over leadership of the camping sector. Product developments included the introduction of a much wider range of destinations both inside and outside France, development of services for children and opening up camp sites for overnight stops. There were also a series of milestones in the development of the business and a number of small competitors were absorbed into the business as the market consolidated. Key events included:

1984 Launch of Eurocamp on the Dutch market
1986 Acquisition of Sunsites and Carefree Camping
1987 Launch of Eurocamp Independent
Take-over of Combined English Stores by Next plc
1988 Launch of Eurocamp on the German market
Management buy-out from Next
1991 Flotation on the London Stock Exchange.

Since flotation the business has continued to develop. The marketing reach of the Eurocamp brand has been extended into several new territories, notably Switzerland, Belgium, Denmark and most recently Poland, whilst customers have increasingly opted for mobile home rather than tent accommodation. From the mid-1990s expansion came through several acquisitions within the holiday sector as well as through organic growth.

1995 Superbreak – leading provider of UK hotel short-breaks acquired

1996 Acquired Camping in Comfort and Tesh Travels–Eurocamp's sales agents in Holland and Germany

1998 Keycamp Holidays – the UK's Number 2 camping and mobile home operator acquired

2000 Explore Worldwide – worldwide adventure holidays specialist acquired

Regal Holidays – scuba diving specialist tour operator acquired

Hotelnet – Internet hotel portal

Rainbow Holidays – UK short-break specialist acquired.

2001 and 2002 have represented a period of greater stability as the company has integrated its purchases into the group and reorganised its management structures. Recent years have seen other important changes. In 1998, after 25 years in Knutsford, the Camping and Group head offices were relocated to a country house at Hartford, near Northwich, Cheshire. The holding company name was also changed from Eurocamp plc to Holidaybreak plc to better reflect the aspirations and range of activities of the group.

Appendix 6.2.3
Profit and Loss Account – Divisional Breakdown

	Camping (£m)	*Hotel breaks (£m)*	*Adventures holidays (£m)*	*Group (£m)*
Turnover				
2001	103.7	57.8	31.0	192.5
2000	102.3	46.1	16.1	164.5
Gross profit				
2001	35.8	11.0	9.2	56.0
2000	34.7	8.7	4.9	48.3
Operating profit				
2001	17.8	5.5	3.4	26.7
2000	17.0	4.4	2.4	23.7

Balance sheet

	Holidaybreak plc Group 2001 (£'000)	*Holidaybreak plc Group 2001 (£'000)*
Fixed Assets		
Intangible assets – goodwill	31,600	32,753
Tangible assets	57,728	53,779
Investments	1,896	1,079
	91,224	87,611
Current assets		
Assets held for disposal	2,626	3,463
Debtors	13,421	12,690
Cash at bank and in hand	49,169	47,803
	65,216	63,956
Creditors		
Amounts falling due within 1 year	(61,925)	(52,553)
Net current assets (liabilities)	3,291	11,403
Total assets less current liabilities	94,515	99,014
Creditors		
Amounts falling due after 1 year	(60,499)	(73,619)
Provisions for liabilities and charges	(6,022)	(5,482)
Net Assets	**27,994**	**19,913**
Capital and reserves		
Called up share capital	2,317	2,290
Reserves	25,677	17,623
Equlty shareholders' funds	**27,994**	**19,913**

Appendix 6.2.4
Operating Divisions of Holidaybreak plc – Background Information

Camping Division

Some 450,000 UK customers (mainly family groups) took a European camping or mobile-home holiday in 1999 in pre-sited accommodation provided by Holidaybreak's various companies or another tour operator. The equivalent figures for the two other most sizeable markets, Holland and Germany, are approximately 250,000 and 150,000 respectively. Holidaybreak customers are generally families from the

ABC1 social categories, or the equivalents in their own countries. The holidays are also popular with couples, particularly at inland destinations outside the school holiday period. Each brand offers a very similar core product. Differentiation is through presentation, distribution and peripheral aspects.

Hotel Breaks Division

Superbreak and its associated brands offer breaks in almost 1400 hotels in the three of five star category throughout the UK. These are featured in catalogue style brochures, which are distributed primarily through UK travel agents. A sustained growth in short-breaks and multiple holiday-taking has been a feature of the UK travel market in recent years. On-line bookings can be made at Superbreak's own site www.superbreak.com. Customers come mainly from the ABC1 social categories. Couples predominate but families are also an important target group. This is a high volume business with relatively low transaction values per booking. Agency commissions, in those cases where they are payable, represent entirely variable costs and no upfront commitments for rooms, transport, theatre tickets etc. are incurred. Fixed costs are very low.

With minimal capital expenditure requirements and year round sales, the business is profitable and cash flows are strong throughout the year. In July 2000 the Internet hotel booking business Hotelnet was acquired. This is one of the leading UK Internet portals for hotel bookings.

Adventure Holidays Division

Explore

Explore offer some 200 winter and summer tours in nearly 100 countries in six continents. Types of tours include:

- *Culture/adventure* – Trips that explore exciting places but do not necessarily involve any particular physical activity, usually focusing on local cultures, historic sites or dramatic locations.

Market Share Estimates (2000)

UK	*Ireland*	*Holland*	*Germany*	*Denmark*	
Holidaybreak	61%	70%	64%	71%	49%
Eurosites (My Travel)	20%	1%	16%	29%	51%
Haven (Bourne Leisure)	10%	12%	8%	–	–
Canvas Holidays	9%	–	13%	–	–
Campotel	–	17%	–	–	–

Sales by brand		*Sales by market*	
Eurocamp	53%	UK/Ireland	68%
Keycamp	38%	Holland	15%
Sunsites	4%	Germany	11%
Independent/other	5%	Others	6%

- *Ethnic or tribal encounters* – Offering the opportunity to meet, and sometimes stay with, traditional local people or tribal groups.
- *Easy to moderate hikes* – A few days easy or moderate walking, usually in open countryside, based in hotel or tented accommodation.
- *Major treks* – This type of trip is recommended to strong mountain walkers who enjoy a challenge. Participants need to be physically fit.
- *Wildlife and natural history* – A particular emphasis on wildlife or natural wonders. Sometimes visiting some of the world's greatest game reserves.
- *Wilderness experience* – Trips that venture into areas where man's influence is limited.
- *Sailtrek/seatrek* – Involving the use of sailboats, ships, ferries or even tallships.
- *Raft or river journeys* – Lasting anything from a few hours to several days. This category includes a wide range of activity type, from whitewater rafting to easy-going cruising and river exploration.

Nearly 80% of Explore's customers come from the UK, booking direct with the company's headquarters in Aldershot.

Overseas customers come mainly from English speaking countries – Australia, New Zealand, Canada, USA, etc. They book through appointed sales agents in those countries. The customers are typically professional people who are reasonably active and want a change from more traditional holiday types. They will often be interested in local cultures and history or wildlife and landscapes. The age profile varies, depending on the tour, but 90% of customers are aged between 25 and 65, with an average age of 44.

Tour costs are largely variable. There are no commitments to airline seats and accommodation costs will depend on the number of travellers in a party. Vehicles and equipment are normally rented locally. Management systems ensure healthy load factors and efficient control of overseas costs. The diversity of the product range and destinations provides considerable resilience and the year-round nature of business (with about 45% of revenues coming in the UK winter period) means that the business is profitable throughout the year. Capital expenditure requirements are limited ensuring strong, year-round cash flows and dollar denominated revenues from overseas customers provide a partial currency hedge.

Regal

Regal Holidays has been arranging diving holidays worldwide since 1987 and is considered to be the UK's leading dive tour operator. Regal offer year-round holidays for both novices and qualified divers. In the 2000/01 brochure there are holidays in 24 destinations, offering over 11 diving activities, plus snorkelling for all ages too. The learn-to-dive market continues to grow and is one in which Regal has been active in developing. There are an increasing number of divers who will take at least two dive holidays per year, one of which would be to a value for money destination such as the Red Sea or a short break in Gozo, and the second one would be to a longer-haul destination such as the Maldives, Grenada etc. The age profile of clients varies but the main sector is aged between 25 and 45 years old. They all tend to be fairly active and want more from their holiday than just a sun tan. Some are dedicated divers who have been diving for years whilst a growing sector are young and single and want to go and learn to dive. Capital expenditure requirements are limited and cash flows are strong year round, allowing for a profitable product throughout the year.

Sources

Company reports – various years; newspaper articles – various.

CASE 3
LEICESTER PROMOTIONS: DESTINATION MANAGEMENT FOR MAXIMISING TOURIST POTENTIAL

An Introduction to Leicester

Leicester is the largest city in England's East Midlands and the tenth largest in the country, with a history dating back to Roman times when it was a strategic stronghold in the control of the Midlands region. It is a major commercial and manufacturing centre, with a thriving ethnic minority drawn from a range of cultural traditions (particularly from the Indian sub-continent), which accounts for over a quarter of Leicester's population. This cultural mix provides opportunities for a wide range of cuisines in the city's many restaurants. Within the city centre there are newly pedestrianised shopping streets, a marketplace which has its origins back through some seven centuries and a modern purpose-built shopping centre. It was also the first British city to be awarded the title of 'Environment City' by the Royal Society for Nature Conservation and the Civic Trust in recognition of the city's pioneering environmental programmes. Tourist attractions include the Leicestershire Museum and Art Gallery, the Haymarket Theatre, (which sometimes hosts shows prior to their West End debut) and the newly completed National Space Centre.

Company Background

Tourism as an area of interest is problematic for many local authorities charged with delivering local government services in the UK. Local areas and communities have often recognised the potential income that can be derived from tourism (both leisure and business related) and in the UK they have traditionally been responsible for providing local tourist information facilities through a network of Tourist Information Centres (TICs). The TICs provide tourism information for visitors and are able to book accommodation but usually have a restricted commercial focus, often limited to selling a narrow range of souvenirs from their offices. Many local authorities have also recognised that tourist related activities can form an important constitutent part of urban renewal. Thus, Liverpool, Cardiff and Edinburgh's waterfront redevelopments, and Birmingham's investment in conference facilities as 'Europe's Meeting Place for example have important tourism components.

However, in terms of direct public spending at the local level, tourism spending has often been small when compared to education and social services and it has sometimes appeared to be low down the pecking order of political issues. Furthermore, decision-making in local authorities, although democratic and accountable, is often slow and lacking entrepreneurial flair. Against this background many cities such as Sheffield, Coventry and Manchester (and some countries) have sought to move the management of tourism outside direct public control through public-private partnerships of various types and configurations.

Leicester Promotions Ltd., the marketing and tourism agency for the City of Leicester, was established in 1993 as a non-profit-making organisation to undertake the marketing and promotion of Leicester with a £1.1 million grant from Leicester City Council. Prior to 1993, tourism promotion services were delivered directly by the city council. With increasing financial pressures and the refocusing of the city council on other services, the delivery of tourism services was transferred out of the public sector. The move from the public sector to the private sector led to dramatic changes in the culture of the organisation and the need to concentrate on activities that were commercially viable. Since 1993 it has become increasingly independent, with less than 50% of its funding coming from Leicester City Council for the year 2001/2.

Business Activities

The principal activity of the company is the marketing and promotion of the City of Leicester and surrounding area and the delivery of tourism services. The company is actively involved in helping the city and country of Leicestershire fulfil their objectives relating to economic growth and social welfare. An objective is to raise the profile of the city, locally, regionally and nationally, and to do so the company specialises in tourism development, marketing and promotion. It aims to balance the delivering of services for local residents with developing the number of visitors to the area.

As partners on the city's key profiling events – Leicester Comedy Festival, Leicester's Diwali celebrations and annual festivals – the company is directly involved in marketing and promotional activities. The marketing and promotional support provided for a major festival 'Festival 2000' was carried out in partnership with the City Council. Direct public relations support was provided to the Comedy Festival and a range of activities was undertaken for the National Space Centre (direct mail, advertising, familiarisation visits and telesales campaigns). Partnerships are undertaken with a wide range of organisations. Other partners include: Leicestershire County Council Tourism Department and many of the city's festivals, local hotels and attractions. Leicester Promotions also continues to be involved in the organisation of the annual Leicester and Leicestershire Tourism Awards. This is done through partnerships with sponsors and it represents a way of recognising and rewarding achievements by venues and attractions around the city and county.

Leicester's Christmas campaigns have proved very successful and have involved partnerships with a number of organisations. The aim has been to promote the city as one of the region's major destinations raising its profile in the region and promoting the Christmas experience of the city to local people. The campaigns have included: producing a TV campaign with The Shires shopping centre and City Centre Management team, producing a 36 page Christmas Guide in partnership with local retailers and the *Leicester Mercury* newspaper, and Leicester on Ice (an outdoor ice rink) as a result of collaboration between an international ice company and sponsorship by GAP.

A further step taken has been the establishment of 'Mosaic' as its in-house marketing communications and design function. Mosaic financially supports the projects Leicester Promotions, continues to undertake as part of its commitment to the city. Clients to date have included both of Leicester's Universities, the National Institute for Adults, Continuing Education, Leicester Festival 2000 and a variety of regeneration projects across the city. As part of regeneration proposals Mosaic has also produced strategic and marketing plans for the run-down Leicester North West area.

Tourist Information Centre (TIC) and UK Holiday Shop

The city councils tourism services are contracted out to Leicester Promotions. As part of their activities they are responsible for the running of Leicester's tourist information centre and they see themselves as offering a leading edge TIC service. The TIC has been awarded the title of Heart of England's Best TIC. The TIC distributes a wide variety of information on attractions, events and hotels and takes bookings for all Leicester's major venues. It is located by the Town Hall and is thus not in a prominent high street position. It has very limited passing trade and they have succeeded in maximising the number of customers despite its disadvantageous position in the city centre. Additionally, it offers a unique UK Holiday Shop and Box Office for local and London events, and also offers ancillary travel services. The other travel agents in the city are clustered together in the main shopping district and the UK Holiday Shop is isolated.

The income received from Leicester City Council is provided directly for information provision activities rather than for retailing or UK Holiday Shop operations. The city council is very clear in its contract with Leicester Promotions that they are divorced from the commercial enterprises of the company. As part of the services delivered to the city council Leicester Promotions represent the council at the Heart of England Tourist Board. They are seen as local authority members in terms of paid subscriptions but their own needs as a commercial marketing and tourism agency may at times be seen as providing points of conflict with their local authority status within the tourist board.

The UK Holiday Shop is the only Association of British Tour Operators (ABTA) bonded travel agency that is part of a tourist information centre and it specialises in UK domestic holiday products racking brochures from a range of tourism suppliers, including the following:

- Blakes
- Box Office (event tickets)
- Country Cottages
- Flightlink
- Haven
- Highlife
- Hoseasons
- Leisure Breaks
- Luxury Hotel Collection
- National Rail
- National Express
- Oasis
- Pontins
- Shearings
- Superbreaks
- Wallace Arnold
- Warner
- Wightlink

The UK Holiday Shop operated in its first year without an ABTA bond and in doing so there were obstacles to its efficient and effective operation as the range of products that could be offered was limited. Difficulties were encountered in setting up agency agreements with tour operators. In explaining to tour operators that they were a TIC there was confusion and suspicion with what that actually meant. For more traditional travel agents there is a good system of support and regular contact but tour operators have not established such links with the UK Holiday Shop. Tour operators are not used to dealing with a travel agent that deals solely with UK domestic holiday products. Administrative working capital problems have arisen from the need to provide cash up front to tour operators without which tour operators would cancel reservations. This has involved a fundamental change in policy, as the inherited local authorities approach (where payments were processed within 30 days) was not an acceptable practice to tour operators. Not only do they have an ABTA bond as a travel agent but they are also required to maintain a bond as a tour operator because Leicester Promotions Ltd. are involved in the packaging of the Leicester tourism product.

Their customers typically take a brochure away and do not necessarily return to them to make a booking. There is no way of recognising that the customer has obtained their holiday brochure from the UK Holiday Shop and that they have actually helped the supplier obtain that booking. Even when customers do book at the UK Holiday Shop return custom is not very common, and they tend to attract customers from the older generations who pay for their holidays with cash. Travel agents located in the high street in Leicester frequently send customers to the UK Holiday Shop as they consider the commission from selling domestic holidays too low to bother with so they would rather pass their custom on. They assure customers that they would get better choice from this alternative shop.

Within the industry a key issue is the low level of commission (usually less than 10%) and how this discourages the selling of the domestic tourism products by travel agents. Domestic tour operators and hoteliers appear to be attempting to decrease commission levels and a number of significant domestic operators (such as Center Parcs, which operates rural activity based holidays) sell directly rather than through agents. The UK Holiday Shop has recently won attention as one of the leading sellers of 'Superbreaks' (a major operator for hotel based UK short breaks).

Appendix 6.3.1
Leicester Promotions Ltd.: Management

Martin Peters, the Managing Director of Leicester Promotions Ltd., has 19 years' experience in tourism and place marketing within both the public and private sectors. On a national level, he is a former Chairman of the 'British Association of Conference Destinations' and remains a director of that Company. He is also a member of the steering group of the British Cities Marketing Board which represents the shared interests of many of the larger British cities. Locally, he has represented Leicester at home and overseas to both the business and leisure tourism markets. In Leicester, he was responsible or introducing the strategies into Leicester's tourist information centre that culminated in the TIC being the first in the country to be awarded ABTA bonding. Formerly Director of Operations, Martin has been with Leicester Promotions since its inception in 1993 and was part of the original team transferred out of the City Council to form the Company.

Martin is supported by a small but enthusiastic team and Leicester Promotions' controlling Board of Directors reflects the city's strengths and diversity. Board members include·

- The Leader of Leicester City Council
- The Chief Executive of Leicester Rugby Club
- The Bishop of Leicester
- The Manager of the Belmont House Hotel.

Appendix 6.3.2
Income and Expenditure Account

	2001 £	*2000* £
Turnover	1,613,807	1,496,785
Operating costs	(1,561,397)	(1,602,435)
Operating surplus/(deficit)	52,410	(105,650)
Surplus/(deficit) on ordinary activities before taxation	56,892	(99,310)
Surplus/(deficit) for the financial year transferred to/(from) reserves	56,041	(95,110)

Operating costs	*2001* £	*2000* £
Promotional costs	147,974	320,665
Tourist information centre costs	361,964	341,206
Conference/tourism costs	73,817	163,955
Rent, rates, heat and light	77,498	44,611
Salaries and national insurance	531,206	498,365
Other operating costs	368,938	233,633

Notes: Transactions with related parties. The company's turnover in 2001 included sales of £839,523 to Leicester City Council. Of this amount £798,000 related to core funding.

Appendix 6.3.3
Tourism Facts and Figures: UK Domestic Tourism

	All tourism trips (millions)	*All tourism nights (millions)*	*Holiday tourism trips (millions)*	*Holiday tourism nights (millions)*	*Holiday tourism spending (£millions)*
1995	121.0	449.8	66.2	302.1	8915
1996	127.0	454.6	64.8	295.8	9365
1997	133.6	473.6	70.8	313.3	10355
1998	122.3	437.6	65.1	284.2	9800
1999	146.1	495.3	75.3	319.6	11095

Sources

Personal interviews.

CASE 4
MYTRAVEL PLC (FORMERLY AIRTOURS): COMPETING IN THE TRAVEL INDUSTRY BIG LEAGUE

An Entrepreneurial Beginning

David Crossland's introduction to the business world was not very promising. On leaving Burnley Grammar School in 1963 he took a job as a glorified coffee boy in a local travel agent and it was difficult to imagine that he would in time become the Chairman of what itself became one of the world's leading travel companies and rank 86th in *The Sunday Times* 'Rich List' of Britain's wealthiest 1000 people. From acorns oak trees grow, and so it was with this Lancastrian entrepreneur.

During the 1970s Crossland developed his own travel agency business, Pendle Travel, together with his brother-in-law Tom Trickett. Entry costs were at the time relatively low and the powerful multiple chains were far less the threat to the independent travel agency business that they were later to become. Trickett backed Crossland in 1972 with an £8000 investment in the first travel agency, and he remained a large shareholder in the Airtours business until the mid-1990s. What later evolved into the MyTravel group emerged with the Airtours name in 1978 when Pendle Travel launched a tour operations division within the successful travel agency business. When the first tours took to the air the company operated from a tiny office above a travel agency in the small Lancashire village of Haslingden. The initial specialisation of the company was low cost package holidays to Malta which found a ready market in north-west England. The speed of development of the tour operating business outstripped that of the travel agency chain and the competitive pressures on independent travel agents were becoming ever greater with 'the march of the multiples' as it was later termed.

From 1985, Crossland, recognising that the development of the business required professional inputs from others, started to draw around him a strong management team to help him build the business. The sale of the 22-branch chain to Hogg Robinson (which operated a nationwide branch network) was concluded in 1986 and in that year Airtours carried 300000 holidaymakers. This period culminated the following year with a major step in the company's strategic development. The company was floated on the London Stock Exchange to become a public limited company (plc), making it one of a very small number of tour operators to have a full stock market listing at that time.

After Flotation

As Airtours plc, the management could raise capital for investment, and although this allowed opportunities for expansion, it also imposed financial disciplines on the management team. As a plc, every move was carefully scrutinised by the City and by the media. The company had to deliver satisfaction to customers, shareholders and bankers, and balancing these competing demands was not always easy. Still based in its north-west England heartland (the company today has its corporate headquarters in the Manchester suburbs), Airtours had established a reputation throughout the travel industry for its relatively low staffing costs and the loyalty it was able to engender in its staff: 'They stay a long time because they are determined that one day they will get to the office before me,' Crossland once joked. Although he became less 'hands-on' as he approached retirement in the late 1990s, he remained as chairman and the days in which he regularly arrived at the office by 5.30 a.m. are still fondly remembered by staff.

Despite many developments in the company, tour operations remained at the core of the group's activities with airline, distribution networks and accommodation developing largely to service the needs of the tour operations activity. The Aspro brand was positioned at the value for money or price-led end of the market while Airtours was positioned as the main market brand with particular appeal to families. A large number of different brochures were produced in the UK using the Airtours name and representing a variety of holiday types. The brochures included: Summer Sun, Far and Away, Turkey, Greece, Florida, Fly-Drive USA, Cruises, Florida and Caribbean Cruise and Stay Holidays (featuring Carnival Cruises), All-Inclusive Suncenters, City and Short Breaks and Lakes and Mountains. The Tradewinds brand offered more exclusive and exotic holidays, mainly utilising scheduled flights to destinations all over the world.

In 1990 Airtours introduced EuroSites by establishing a subsidiary operating self-drive holidays with pre-arranged camping locations. By the late 1990s EuroSites had become the second largest company (after Eurocamp) in this area of the market. EuroSites offered tent and mobile home holidays across Europe, selling since its launch in the UK and more recently in the Dutch and German markets. Further capacity was added progressively from one season to the next through the adding of capacity at sites and by adding additional camp sites to its portfolio. Demand for the product proved to be strong with good levels of profitability, high levels of customer satisfaction and high levels of repeat business. During 1990 'The Cottage Directory' product selling UK country cottages was also developed. However, sales levels achieved were lower than forecast and the product proved operationally difficult, involving as it did close liaison with a large number of individual property owners and a comparatively low value of sales per brochure page. After the end of its first season an offer for the business was received and accepted, thereby incurring a relatively limited loss overall.

Throughout the 1990s, the UK outbound tour-operating sector was characterised by intense competition and was highly seasonal and cyclical in its booking patterns. A number of factors combined to create a substantial imbalance between supply and demand for the summer of 1995. Tour operators had anticipated the arrival of the much talked about 'feel good factor' in the UK economy and sales in the pre-Christmas selling period were encouraging. However, this did not continue into the peak booking months of January – March and all operators maintained capacity in the expectation of an upturn in demand. Several companies also declared their aim of gaining market share in 1995. Onto this market position was added the effect of the excellent, record-breaking UK weather during the summer months. With supply greater than demand in the increasingly important 'late sales' market, many prices fell to unprofitable levels across the industry and discounting was substantially higher than in most years.

The alternatives indicated by the 1995 market were straightforward. The industry could either downsize by offering fewer holidays at realistic margins or continue on the same basis as pre-1995 with higher and higher late sales discounts giving customers little incentive to book early.

Launched ahead of schedule on 18th March, 1991, Airtours International was set up. Unlike some other charter carriers, Airtours International's airline capacity was intended solely to serve the group's tour operations. Its capacity was fully utilised on Airtours business and was not dependent upon third party customers. The growing needs of the Airtours' tour operations required assurance that sufficient seat capacity could be acquired at the right price and of a consistent quality. The airline's growth, however, was limited by Airtours' winter tour operations since it was during the winter that any excess charter capacity was likely to become apparent. With this factor in mind, the airline provided over 90% of the winter tour operations flying programme, dropping to between 60 and 70% for the summer programme.

Airtours' northern roots were emphasised by the position of Manchester airport. In 1986, 76% of Airtours bookings were for Manchester departures and although growth from the airport continued in terms of absolute numbers, its relative position declined since it represented only 46% of UK departures in 1991 and this proportion subsequently fell further. The company's in-house airline, Airtours International, was, from its inception in 1991, based at the airport.

In September 1992 Airtours re-entered the UK retail travel agency business with the purchase of 335 branches of the third largest retail chain, Pickfords. This was followed by the purchase in June 1993 of 210 branches acquired from Hogg Robinson, moving the group to second position behind Lunn Poly in UK retail distribution. The branches served as outlets for the distribution of Airtours products and importantly provided market intelligence on customer preferences and market trends. A major re-branding exercise took place during December 1993 in which the division was re-launched under the Going Places name. Within seven days every one of the company's 545 retail shops had been fitted out with new fascias, signage and stationery. Later in the year, the 40 strong Winston Rees chain was added to the Airtours network.

The merging of the large retail networks inevitably resulted in a degree of duplication with some shops being closer to others than would be considered ideal. Little merit was seen in closing branches despite the close proximity of a second Going Places outlet as long as each shop continued to make a satisfactory contribution to central overheads. Nevertheless, the profitability of each shop was continually reviewed and while many new sites were subsequently developed by Going Places, several poorly performing shops were closed and sold off. In 1995 Going Places had over 650 branches operating the UK compared to 795 operated by Lunn Poly the market leader. Late Escapes, a telephone sales business specialising in the sales of holidays within eight weeks of departure, was purchased in 1994. Late Escapes, based in north-east England, made extensive use of the teletext information services for the marketing of its services directly to customers in their homes.

In January 1993 Airtours launched a hostile take-over bid for Owners Abroad (later known as First Choice Holidays), another large tour operator, which served many of the same destinations. The acrimonious battle fought over several months and widely reported by the media led to a narrow defeat for Airtours and incurred costs of some £9 million.

International Expansion

After 1994 the group expanded internationally, most significantly in Scandinavia and subsequently in North America. The acquisition from Scandinavian Airways in June 1994 of the Scandinavian Leisure Group (SLG) gave Airtours ownership of the largest leisure travel company in Scandinavia, albeit one that served many of the same destinations as Airtours in the UK market. SLG operates the Ving, Always and Saga brands, with particular strengths in Norway and Sweden. Seventy per cent of its sales were made directly to public either by 'direct sell' methods or through dedicated retail outlets with the remaining 30% of bookings being made through third party travel agents.

During the winter of 1994/95 SLG undertook a major restructuring exercise of its operations which together with an improvement in the Scandinavian economies resulted in a greatly enhanced performance by this division. SLG carried 915000 customers in 1995 increasing to 1028000 in 1996. The acquisition of the Spies group, Scandinavia's third largest tour operator during 1996, added a further 397000 customers under the Spies and Tjaerborg brands. The Spies group was extensively reorganised and re-focused on acquisition with most administrative functions being integrated into SLG's Stockholm headquarters and respective overseas resort offices being rationalised. Following its major expansion SLG had approximately 50% of the Scandinavian market with the leading position in each of the Scandinavian countries. The acquisition of Spies gave Airtours full control of Scandinavia's largest charter airline Premiair.

The Scandinavian acquisitions brought with them hotel and holiday complex portfolios of 16 properties in the case of SLG and 25 properties in the case of Spies, located in many of the principal resorts served by the group's tour operations. Accommodation ownership allowed retention within the group of a higher proportion of resort expenditure and allowed the company to more accurately monitor customer tastes and preferences. By limiting hotel ownership to less than 20% of total accommodation requirements within any one area, the group was able to ensure high occupancy levels. Distinct accommodation brands were developed in order to satisfy the differing demands of the group's tour operations. The successful Sunwing brand was primarily designed for Scandinavian customers, whilst the Suncenter product was marketed through Airtours Holidays and catered largely for the needs of the UK market. Suncenters offered families an action packed home-from-home with many activities, lots of entertainment and children's clubs.

The acquisition of Sunquest Vacations in August 1995 established Airtours' presence in the North American market through its tour operating businesses in Ontario and Western Canada and this was followed by the acquisition in August of Alba, another significant Canadian tour operator, in August of the following year. Airtours also made its first foray into the vast US market during 1996, deciding that the most cost effective entry vehicle would be through a 'greenfield' start-up operation capitalising on the Sunquest brand name. Accordingly, Sunquest Holidays was formed under the leadership of John Trickett, who had previously held management positions within the Airtours Group in the UK prior to moving to California in 1989 where he had subsequently worked for other tour operators. The company operated its first programme of holidays in 1997, flying largely from California and focusing on Mexico, the Caribbean and Hawaii, all of which were also served by existing tour operations within the Airtours group. In 1996 Airtours' North American Leisure Group had built a business carrying almost 500000 customers a year.

Cruising as a holiday choice grew in popularity during the 1990s in most Western economies. The UK market was still relatively small (representing about 500000 customers in 1994) due to its image of high cost, exclusivity and older age group appeal, but this market doubled in size between 1994 and 2000. It also grew elsewhere in Europe but accounted for only 2% of European package holidays as at the year 2000. The North American cruise market developed in a different way with rapid growth in the later 1990s, a much younger customer base, specialist targetted cruise programmes and a product that offered high standards at competitive prices.

In 1994 Airtours created a cruise product, Sun Cruises, at a price level that would appeal to its existing customer base, and two ships containing a total of 1900 berths were purchased. Passengers flew from local airports in the UK, Scandinavia and North America to their point of embarkation (mainly in traditional Mediterranean resort areas and the Caribbean). The operational management of the ships was sub-contracted to an experienced cruise operator. Utilising many of the services of the group's tour operating businesses and taking advantage of its distribution network substantially reduced costs and enabled a high quality product to be offered at prices significantly below those offered by traditional cruise operators. In only its second year of operation Sun Cruises achieved load factors approaching 100% and a UK market share of 18%.

The principal, risks usually perceived by external observers of the travel industry for a group such as Airtours are those of under-utilised aircraft and excess hotel accommodation for which payment has already been made. The reality was that Airtours, in common with other major tour operators, had considerable flexibility in its contracting of both of these services. Aviation contracts with third party suppliers usually had a variety of cancellation options, which could be exercised once booking patterns have been established. This provided a margin of comfort when coupled with the way in which Airtours' in-house flying capacity was tailored to provide 60–70% of expected summer requirements. With regard to accommodation, only 10% of Airtours' requirements were booked on an irrevocable basis.

Perhaps more critical to the business, and common to other businesses dealing with international conditions, were changes in exchange and interest rates and aviation fuel. Airtours developed a policy of 'hedging' against all major risks on the financial and commodity markets prior to each brochure launch. Specifically, the group developed the practice of negotiating a range of forward contracts and options. In this way the costs of hedging these risks were built into the brochure selling prices.

The holiday business is well-known for generating substantial cash flows as customers traditionally pay in advance and the holiday companies pay their suppliers in arrears. There is a degree of seasonality to this cash flow but even at its lowest point, substantial cash balances are usually held by the tour operating companies. Effective 'cash management' of these balances therefore became a very important part of managing the business and interest receivable, as, with other tour operators, this represented a significant source of income. Surplus funds were placed on deposit with established international banks, but other investment opportunities were examined at times of falling interest rates.

Airtours – Competing in the Big League

For many years Airtours was seen as the darling of the City – a travel company that was professionally run and which reported steadily increasing turnover and profits. Its shares peaked at 540 pence in mid- 1999 but then languished at prices of between 200 and 300 pence as a series of problems beset the company over 2000 and 2001. Europewide consolidation of the sector led to the emergence of powerful new competitive groupings while its own deals largely failed to impress. The years 1998 and 1999 saw a flurry of take-over activity in the UK tour operating sector with Airtours and other large groups consolidating their leading positions following a Monopolies and Merger Commission (now the UK Competition Commission) investigation. Thus, Airtours added to its portfolio of activities by acquiring medium sized British operators (such as Cresta, Bridge, Panorama and Direct Holidays and the Bridge Travel Group) whilst Thomson added Crystal Holidays, and First Choice added Unijet.

Problems began for the group in 1999 when Airtours bought Travelworld, a 120 strong Yorkshire based travel agency for £12 million. Airtours had to beat off competition from rival companies to buy Travelworld, and post acquisition it re-branded the shops and bolted them on to its existing Going Places chain. Travelworld's financial position was less robust than it had been hoped at the time of the purchase and this raised questions about Airtours' management's astuteness in making the deal. Of greater strategic significance to the group however was the impact of the consolidation that swept through the sector.

'Scale matters in a business where the better performers only make a 4% profit margin,' said John Donaldson, Thomas Cook chief executive. 'If you can get cost efficiencies of 1 to 2 per cent through better buying, such as hotel rooms and aircraft fuel, that has a very material impact on profitability. That's, what's driving consolidation.' Tour operating has always been viewed as a risky business where most profits are made during a short summer period. The tour operators responded to this in several ways. In the 1990s the sector increasingly became vertically integrated and horizontal expansion followed, first at the national level and then internationally when domestic opportunities became more limited. The new century, however has been characterised not by the largest players purchasing smaller, weaker rivals, but by consolidation among the largest players themselves, which has seen the emergence of four key groups: Preussag and Thomas Cook based in Germany and Airtours and First choice based in the UK.

The shape of the European industry was largely determined at corporate headquarters in Toronto, Canada and Hanover in Germany by the changing strategies of two large industrial companies. Thomson, the Canadian media group, withdrew from the sector by floating its Thomson Holiday group in the UK during 1998. Preussag AG, a German industrial and logistics group, decided to withdraw from these sectors in order to concentrate its activities on the travel industry. In 1999 Preussag purchased Germany's largest travel group (TUI) and followed up this purchase a year later with the acquisition of Thomson Travel. The TUI purchase left Preussag with a stake in Thomas Cook, a first class brand name in the travel industry. European Community rules meant that the Thomas Cook holding had to be sold by Preussag when Thomson was subsequently purchased. C&N Touristic, Germany's second largest tour operating group (which was owned jointly by Lufthansa and Karstadt, a department store group) subsequently purchased Thomas Cook and later changed its name to Thomas Cook AG.

Airtours purchased its means of entry into the German market in 1998 when it purchased a minority stake in Frosch Touristik International (FTI). Germany's fourth ranked tour operating group. That sun-starved Germany and Britain emerged to dominate the industry in Europe is not surprising. They are the two largest European markets, with the Germans, who typically have six weeks annual holiday, spending £40 billion on international tourism – 20% more than the British figure. Airtours, however, in common with other British companies expanding in Germany, found the going difficult. Airtours discovered it had bought trouble in that the 2000 season produced losses of some £100 million for FTI, which resulted in Airtours taking full control of the company in late 2000. The difficulties were attributed to the overestimation of capacity requirements for the summer season and being left with unfilled allocations.

Although (as at 2002) further consolidation remained likely, there were legal constraints upon further consolidation. In 1999 Airtours' £950 million bid for First Choice plc was blocked by the European Commission on the grounds that it would have left three vertically integrated tour operators (Thomson, Airtours and Thomas Cook) controlling over 80% of some short-haul tour operating destinations. Although Airtours did not rule out a further bid in the future, and lodged an appeal against the decision, First Choice emerged reinvigorated having modified its strategic positioning. First Choice's emphasis began to shift away from high volume; low margin businesses towards a portfolio of individually branded more specialist products offering potentially higher returns. Nevertheless, cost efficiency was maintained through the utilisation of centralised systems and corporate buying power.

The vertically integrated model whereby a single group became the full owner (or had equity in) airline operations, tour operations and travel retailing was, however the subject of further development. Until the mid to late 1990s most groups avoided investment in accommodation, believing that the high capital costs and inherent interest rate and property risks involved were at variance with the type of businesses they had traditionally run. Competition from operators around Europe, the growth of new markets in Eastern and Central Europe, and a slow-down in the rate of new building led to a shortage of good quality accommodation at key resorts (particularly in the Balearic and Canary Islands). The shortage increasingly led to a reassessment of the position with regard to property and hotel ownership on the part of the big travel groups.

Airtours became hoteliers with the purchase of Scandinavian Leisure Group and then further embraced accommodation ownership with the purchase of several hotels and apartment complexes. In January 2000, for example, the company purchased for £63.4 million the Bellevue apartments, Europe's largest complex situated in Majorca. This not only gave the company access to high quality accommodation in an important location, but it also denied others such access at a time when increasingly stringent planning procedures prevented large scale new developments.

In 1997 Airtours and Carnival Cruise Line (the world's largest) agreed to jointly purchase the Costa cruise line based in Florida at a cost (to Airtours) of £59 million. Sales through Airtours' distribution network were significant but far from spectacular and the sale of the assets to the partner Carnival in summer 2000 for £350 million represented an opportunity to realise the value of a non-core asset at a time when a large amount of additional cruising capacity was about to enter the market. The transaction left Airtours better positioned to exploit its business model in Europe and North America and to seek investments, which would further support and enhance the group's core activities.

Management, Staff and Systems

The transition from its single business core of tour operating into an integrated international travel business was rapid, and this placed considerable demands on management, staff and systems. Considerable resources were devoted to staff recruitment, management training and the procurement of the necessary computer hardware and software in order to enhance the group's competitive position. As at the year 2002, Airtours, now renamed the MyTravel group, was managed on a decentralised basis with a small head office team and a separate Board of Directors for each of the main divisions: UK Tour Operations, UK Retail, Scandinavian Leisure Group, North American Leisure Group, Aviation division, and Cruise and Hotels division.

Such rapid development did not always run smoothly. Airtours was a long-time favourite target for attacks by sections of the media, attracting poor ratings by reports from The Consumers' Association, and attracting more than its share of press criticism over quality standards. During the late 1990s, Airtours made strenuous efforts to ensure that customers knew what they were buying and that they got what they were promised. Each of the group's divisions operated its own quality control initiatives relying heavily on customer feed-back, and although it remained an area for some concern relative to competitors, there was a marked reduction in the proportion of complaints relative to holidays sold.

Management clashes led to a series of high profile departures from Airtours. A new director was brought from a cinema chain to shake up the UK Retail division during 2000, and subsequently sacked five directors of Going Places. The sacked directors launched actions in the High Court to recover money they claimed they were owned with two of them later being re-employed by First Choice plc. Meanwhile at the group level, Harry Coe and Hugh Collinson, longstanding board members and Airtours' founder David Crossland's 'right hand men', both retired. Perhaps the most damaging, however, was the defection and two senior executives during 2001 to arch-rival, Thomson.

The imponderable factor for all firms was the future of direct dealings with customers as opposed to dealings through intermediaries such as travel agents. Airtours invested heavily in call centres, and channels such as TV text services and TV channels dedicated to travel grew in importance, but capturing e-commerce business remained the elusive prize. Airtours chief executive Tim Byrne hoped to make huge savings by persuading people to book direct rather than on the High Street. Just two years after a big UK retail expansion (of Going Places) he closed 120 of 867 shops in 2001, and more were expected to follow. Airtours struck a £20 million deal with TV text service. Teletext to distribute holidays on digital channels, but it was the £240 million purchase of US Travel Services International (which included mytravel.com) in 2000, which was viewed as the key deal in distribution.

The acquisition brought expenditure by Airtours on its net strategy to more than £340 million, with few discernible signs of success. The MyTravel brand was launched in Autumn 2001 and was rolled out across the shops and brochures to raise visibility. The Airtours name had served the group well and continued to be the largest tour-operating brand, Airtours Holidays, but it was thought that benefits could be gained from aligning the plc name with the new branded distribution. The new name was placed on each of the 115 million brochures produced each year, the 1000 retail outlets and on each piece of stationery.

Although it cost 15% of turnover to book through travel agents and just 5% online everything hung on persuading people to book their holidays in the way. Consumer purchasing behaviour was deeply embedded and slow to change. Travel agents, like shoe shops, were often found clustered on a high street allowing comparisons to be made and bargains to be struck by customers. Going to buy the holiday was associated with the excitement of the holiday itself and so the change to online booking was not expected to be fast growing. Internet bookings struggled to get off the ground in the UK as elsewhere, with, as at 2002, package holidays bought in this way only accounting for 1% of business.

Appendix 6.4.1
MyTravel Plc Group Structure (2002)

	Markets			
Products	United Kingdom	Scandinavia	Germany	North America
Distribution	Going Places Late Escapes MyTravel	Spies Tjaerborg Ving Shops MyTravel	Fti Touristik	World Choice Travel MyTravel Cruises Only
Tour Operations	Airtours Aspro Tradewinds EuroSites Direct Holidays Manos Panorama Cresta	Ving Always Saga Spies Tjaerborg	Fti Touristik	Sunquest Vacations AlbaTours Vacation Express
Aviation	Airtours International	Premiair		Skyservice*
Cruise and Hotels	Resort Hotels: Sunwing, Tenerife Sol†, Hotetur† Cruise: Sun Cruises			

*Long-term contract.

†Joint ventures.

Note: The Board of Directors comprises the Chairman (David Crossland), Chief Executive (Tim Byrne) the group finance director, chairmen of the operating divisions (UK Leisure Group, Scandinavian Leisure Group, German Leisure Group, MyTravel North America and the Aviation Division) and three non-executive directors. Each operating division had its own directors chaired by a main board member.

Appendix 6.4.2
Some comments on David Crossland – MyTravel Chairman

Speaking in 1992 Chairman David Crossland said, 'I certainly can't claim that I sat down 20 years ago and created a master plan for a travel business, but I did always believe that if you really wanted to achieve something you could.' From the earliest days, Crossland wanted to give holidaymakers a good value-for-money product and believed that if they received such a product that they would come back for more. That desire is something that has not changed and it proved to be correct. He recently said that '[the only people] I really worry about are those who buy our products, the end users. I care passionately about them.'

Initially, Airtours was very much a family business. It had very little capital and Crossland knew the only way the company would grow was through reinvestment and hard work. Today it is a big organisation, but Crossland argues that the management and staff all share that original commitment towards passengers and they work extremely hard and show great loyalty. 'My enthusiasm seems to be infectious and rubs off on them,' he said 'It is still a family business, but now it has become the Airtours family rather than the Crossland family.'

Crossland has said that he only really has one talent and that is the ability to appoint managers who are far cleverer than he is – people who are extremely professional and absolute experts in their fields. The success of the company has a great deal to do with them. Another key to the success, he said was that 'we believe in our product. We believe we have a really good product, that our brochures are clear, clean and easily understood, and that our advertising is effective. We have grown and changed, but our roots are in travel retailing and we understand, from inside knowledge, just how retailers work.'

In 2002 David Crossland appointed Tim Byrne, Airtours' managing director, as chief executive to oversee the day-today running of the company. Crossland's plan was then to concentrate on exploring new opportunities. This came in the wake of news that Airtours' underlying profits had fallen 30% against the previous year. Pre-tax profits were up to £211.4m from £125.9m, but the problem with FTI, its German business (which lost £100m during these two years) is still being addressed. MyTravel's mistake was entering the German market with a minority stake. It acquired control only during 2001, but not in time to reverse the damage caused by excess capacity in the local holiday market. Yet Crossland saw the problems as a blip: 'You've got to get it into perspective,' he said. 'When we floated in 1987 we were making £2m and when we started we employed two people.'

A key mistake was made in 1999 when the company thought it was taking a low-risk route by only buying 30% of FTI but it actually turned out to be worse because, in Crossland's words, 'We did not have control and if we had had control this year, which has been a difficult year in the German market, the losses would not have been as bad.' Airtours finally took full control of FTI in September 2001 and big changes were made in the German subsidiary. Overseas bed rates were renegotiated using the MyTravel bargaining strength, the cost of sales were brought down and the company was restructured. Crossland added that 'it grew very fast. It had an entrepreneur who would not take advice about putting a structure in and was trying to manage all the divisions himself.'

Having been the driving force behind MyTravel's growth and then the architect of its move into Germany, Crossland's challenge became to restore investor confidence. It has been suggested that MyTravel is a one-man band, but Crossland responds by saying that 'we have some strong managers and directors who run big businesses all over the world . . . but I'm the front person and take responsibility when we have a difficult year.' The appointment of Tim Byrne was clearly important for the group; as Crossland explained, 'We need one guy sitting on the top of each division and driving out the costs and sweeping the synergies across the matrix rather than just down it. It will leave me able to spot opportunities, which is what I'm good at.'

Appendix 6.4.3
Statement from Airtours 1996 Report and Accounts

Three years ago we concluded that in order to maintain our rate of growth we would need to develop our business overseas. At that time we stated our objectives of achieving, in the medium term, an even split of profits between UK and overseas businesses.

In a short period of time, Airtours has transformed itself from a purely UK based company into an internationally diversified leisure group which is now the largest air inclusive tour operator in the world. The growth of the group continues to produce economies of scale and by managing capacity across our different markets we obtain the maximum utilisation of our aircraft, cruise ships and hotels.

For future growth we shall seek to develop or acquire businesses operating in markets which we understand, where we can add value and where the acquired business has high quality management or alternatively can be readily integrated into our existing management infrastructures.

Appendix 6.4.4
Statement from Airtours 2001 Report and Accounts

Reorganisation and Consolidation

The consolidation of the major UK tour operator into a single site in Rochdale has been successfully implemented and the reorganisation of Scandinavian businesses from a brand based to a country based organisation was completed in early 2001. The most dramatic changes were seen within the German business. A new management team was put in place and the complete reorganisation led to significant reductions in the German workforce as efficiencies were identified. The closure of the dedicated charter carrier FlyFTi will result in significant savings going forward. The consolidation of the

North American charter operations under the Airtours North America name was also completed.

Operational Flexibility

The business model favoured by MyTravel ensures inherent flexibility to deal with capacity reductions. The under-sizing of the aircraft fleet and to an even greater extent hotels and cruising ensures capacity can be reduced to meet market conditions without significant exposure to the costs associated with under-utilised assets. Overcapacity in distribution however enables the group to widen its product offerings through featuring favoured products provided by third parties.

Appendix 6.4.5
Tui AG

According to Dr. Michael Frenzel, the boss of German holiday giant Preussag, the package tour must become more European. Although there will still be room for diversity and differences in national tastes will still be important, Preussag believes that further integration at a European level will take place. Preussag's £1.8 billion takeover of Thomson Travel in August 2000 made it the largest package holiday firm in the world. Frenzel's opinion is one that cannot be ignored.

Frenzel, 53, manages Preussag from an austere headquarters in Hanover, where for the past six years he has plotted the company's transformation from an industrial conglomerate into a more focused package holiday giant. After joining the company in 1994, Frenzel has embarked on a high-risk strategy. While rapidly withdrawing from the group's poorly performing industrial interests, he has set about acquiring prized assets amongst European holiday companies. As an industrial group there were about 50 separate businesses but importantly Preussag were not number one at anything.

Leisure and tourism presented major opportunities for growth. Rivals cannot help but admire the single-mindedness demonstrated in his plans for the tour group. In 1998, the German travel giant Tui and airline Hapag-Lloyd were acquired, followed by British holiday and financial services group Thomas Cook. Then, after acquiring a couple of travel agency chains, Frenzel went for his holiday dream in the form of Thomson Travel. He snatched it at the eleventh hour from C&N Touristic, Germany's second-biggest travel company. He had promised to turn Thomas Cook into the British market leader ahead of Thomson and Airtours (MyTravel), but sold Thomas Cook to another German tour operator as soon as Thomson came on the market. Thomson represented the bigger opportunity.

Control of two of the UK's biggest tour companies make the two German operators the two most powerful holiday firms in Europe. This is all a far cry from just a few years ago, when British firms such as MyTravel were homing in on German companies. After a period of aggressive selling and buying Tui as it is now called is concentrating on digesting and integrating the companies. Twelve teams of executives have been established to ease the integration of the various new companies in what has been dubbed Operation Titan.

'It's not a question of cost savings,' Frenzel maintains 'it's about being more flexible in our destinations, in buying fuel for our airlines and negotiating on hotel beds. Shifting over-capacity of tourists from one subsidiary's resort to another to take advantage of synergies also offers opportunities.'

Appendix 6.4.6
MyTravel in the Wake of the 11 September, 2001 Terrorist Attacks

The large tour operators faced a difficult situation in the wake of the 11 September terrorist strikes. The events caused early bookings for summer 2002 to crash by between 30 and 40 per cent. However, instead of the lean pickings which many experts predicted for tour operators, swift and firm action restored 2002's profit prospects. In an industry often criticised for targetting market share over profitability, the events of 11 September provide an illustration of the vulnerability of the industry to external shocks, whilst the events following the attacks show a new willingness amongst managers to target profitability by cutting capacity.

After 11 September, the large tour operators cut (by about 15%) the number of holidays and aircraft seats they were willing to supply to the UK market for the 2002 season. At the same time research predicted a strong recovery in customer booking. By cutting supply while demand remained strong, holiday prices remained firm, boosting yields and profits. For investors used to seeing the holiday companies swamp the market with cheap deals to drive market share rather than earnings, this was good news. A study by the Centre for Economic Business Research into the impact of 11 September and subsequent conflicts suggested that a 5 per cent reduction in demand for overseas holidays was likely, which means the industry's capacity cuts more than compensate.

Appendix 6.4.7
MyTravel – Financial Statements

MyTravel – Financial summary (1986 – 2001)

	2001	2000	1999	1998	1997	1996	1995	1994	1993	1992	1991	1990	1989	1988	1987	1986
Turnover (£m)	5061.4	3949.0	3309.3	2753.4	2235.6	1717.9	1317.8	971.7	615.6	405.6	289.5	183.0	155.6	102.5	68.3	55.0
Profit before tax (£m)	81.3	211.4	125.9	125.7	117.2	86.8	59.1	75.8	45.6	36.5	27.5	6.3	5.2	4.1	2.0	2.0
Earnings per ordinary share	6.28p	35.98p	19.74p	21.14p	20.62p	45.63p	32.76p	41.79p	29.22p	24.47p	24.68p	6.69p	5.12p	17.43p	8.55p	8.53p
Dividends per ordinary share	9.50p	9.00p	8.25p	7.50p	6.67p	16.00p	14.00p	12.00p	9.00p	7.25p	5.75p	2.03p	1.72p	6.25p	n/a	n/a
No. of employees	27868	24316	20226	17354	14565	12198	9896	6337	3819	1349	946	571	389	310	212	283

MyTravel – Business Segment Analysis

		Turnover (£m)		Profits before tax (£m)		Net assets (£m)	
		2001	2000	2001	2000	2001	2000
UK	Continuing	2672.2	2323.8	110.6	279.9	106.9	282.6
Other Europe	Continuing					286.5	273.3
	Scandinavia and Netherlands	1018.3	926.8	31.2	20.7		
	FTi	684.4	92.8	–52.6	–13.3		
	Acquisitions	14.0	–	0.8	–		
	Discontinued	22.3	143.3	–2.0	–36.1		
North America	Continuing	641.8	462.8	–10.8	–19.3	128.5	–12.3
	Acquisitions	8.4	–	–	–		
Joint Ventures	Continuing						
	FTi	–	293.9	–	–49.6		
	Other	28.1	8.5	4.1	2.2		
	Discontinued						
	Costa Cruises	–	183.4	–	26.9		
Total		5089.5	4435.3	81.3	211.4	521.4	543.6

Appendix 6.4.7
MyTravel – Financial Statements – *continued*

MyTravel Balance Sheet		*2001*	*2000*	*1999*	*1998*	*1997*
Fixed assets	Tangible	431.1	513.5	417.8	310.7	261.4
	Intangible	540.2	534.8	36.9	–	–
	Investments	83.7	55.3	116.9	82.7	63.0
	Total	1055.0	1103.6	571.6	393.4	324.4
Current assets	Stock	13.3	17.2	11.4	17.0	6.4
	Debtors	838.5	712.2	550.5	403.5	331.7
	Investments	0	0	0	0	0
	Bank and Deposits	378.6	793.3	554.2	364.2	406.6
	Total	1230.4	1522.7	1116.1	784.7	744.7
Current liabilities	Creditors	–359.0	–462.6			
	Loans/overdraft	–16.9	–33.8			
	Other	–827.4[a]	–777.5[a]			
	Total	–1203.3	–1273.9	–948.8	–802.0	–747.2
Non-current liabilities		–560.2	–695.4	–490.8	–210.1	–562.6
Total assets less liabilites		521.9	543.6	248.1	166.0	240.7
Shareholders funds	Share capital	49.3	49.1	47.8	47.5	47.2
	Reserves	263.0	285.7	200.3	118.5	193.5
Non-equity preference shares		209.6	208.8	–	–	–
	Total	521.9	543.6	248.1	166.0	240.7

Notes: [a]Of which Revenue received in advance = 310.8 (2001) 366.4 (2002) and Accruals and deferred income = 330.2 (2001), 250.5 (2000).

Appendix 6.4.8
Major Competitors – Financial Statements

Major competitors – turnover and profits

		2000	*1999*
Turnover	Tui (Euro m)	21,854.0	16,501.0
	of which tourism (Euro m)	10,562.1	7,164.8
	F Choice (£m)	1,880.7	1,465.8
	Thomas Cook (DM m)	9,740.8	9,073.9
Profit Before Tax	Tui (Euro m)	402.5	354.4
	of which Tourism (Euro m)	423.3	307.5
	F Choice (£m)	68.9	38.0
	Thomas Cook (DM m)	220.4	209.5

Note: Euro/£ = 1.65, DM/$ = 3.20, $/£ = 1.40

Balance Sheet First Choice Holidays plc (£M)

		2000	*1999*	*1998*	*1997*	*1996*
Fixed assets	Tangible					
	Intangible					
	Investments					
	Total	462.1	134.3	58.3	51.3	58.9
Current assets	Stock					
	Debtors					
	Investments					
	Bank and Deposits					
	Prepayments					
	Total	704.9	417.6	380.9	264.4	238.5
Current liabilities	Creditors					
	Loans/overdraft					
	Other					
	Total	–660.1	–375.2	–325.4	–227.2	–206.2
Non-current liabilities		–89.6	–57.5	–45.7	–28.1	–30.8
Total assets less liabilities		417.3	119.2	68.1	60.4	60.4
Shareholders funds	Share capital	213.2	13.1	13.1	13.1	7.1
	Reserves	204.1	106.1	55.0	47.3	53.3
	Total	417.3	119.2	68.1	60.4	60.4

Note: Royal Caribbean Cruise Lines invested £200 million in a strategic alliance with First Choice during 2000. The alliance provides the cruise line with a 20% stake and enhanced distribution whilst providing First Choice with access to high quality cruising products.

Sources

Company reports – various years; newspaper articles – various.

CASE 6.5
COMPETITIVE STRATEGY AT RYANAIR

The Launch and Early Development

Ryanair, now firmly established as Europe's largest low fares airline, began operations back in 1985 with the launch of a daily flight on a 15 seater turbo prop aircraft between Waterford Airport in the south east of Ireland and London Gatwick. The company had a commitment to low fare air travel and making air travel affordable for people in Ireland and the UK, but in the early years problems were encountered in delivering this commitment. In the company's first year, its 57 employees carried just over 5000 passengers on its one route. In 1986, Ryanair broke the high fare cartel, which was then operated by the two state airlines. Aer Lingus and British Airways, on the Dublin–London route. The Dublin–London route had stagnated at about 1 million passengers per annum between 1975 and 1985, and was then characterised by some of the highest air fares in Europe. Prior to Ryanair, the normal air fare between Dublin and London in 1985 was £209 return. Ryanair began services on the 23rd May, 1986 with two turbo prop BA 748 aircraft and an introductory launch fare of £94.99 return. Ryanair was the first European airline specifically set up to offer low fares on short-haul intra-European routes.

Over the next three years (1987 – 89) Ryanair expanded rapidly, opening many new routes between Ireland and the UK, increasing the fleet by adding BAC 1–11 jets, and ATR 42 turbo prop aircraft. Whilst customers continued to flock to Ryanair for the low airfares, costs were not controlled, and the company continued to rack up losses. By 1989, the company employed 350 people, operated 14 aircraft (four different types), was carrying 600000 passengers a year, but had managed to lose £20m in just four years.

New Management Team

Under a new management team, a major overhaul of the airline was undertaken in 1990/91, with Ryanair relaunched as the first of a new breed of 'low fares/no frills' airline. In relaunching the airline in this way, the management was adapting the formula so successfully pioneered by South-west Airlines in the USA in the period since deregulation of the American aviation market in 1978. Non-profitable routes were eliminated, the network was cut back from nineteen to only five routes, the turbo prop aircraft were disposed of and air fares across the remaining network were substantially reduced with 70% of all seats offered at the two lowest fares. On Dublin–London, for example, a new promotional fare of just £69 return was launched which stimulated a whole new era of growth for Ryanair. By 1991, Ryanair was operating an all-jet fleet of 6 BAC 1–11 aircraft, employing 350 people, carrying 700000 passengers on just five routes, and it had recorded its first ever profit (despite the damage done to the airline industry by the Gulf War in 1991).

Over the next couple of years, schedules on the key Dublin–London route were increased, average air fares were lowered, new routes were launched from Dublin to Birmingham, Glasgow, Manchester and Gatwick, while traffic continued to grow strongly. By 1994, Ryanair was employing over 500 people, carrying over 1.5 million passengers per annum, offering lower than ever air fares of just £49 return on the Dublin–London route, and it recorded its fourth continuous year of profitability. In 1994 also came the acquisition of Ryanair's first Boeing 737 aircraft, with an order for six 737–200 series aircraft (130 seats) being purchased direct from Boeing. Over the following three years a further 15,737–200 aircraft were purchased, bringing the fleet to 21,737–200s. To coincide with this expansion of the fleet, many more new routes were opened by Ryanair between Ireland and the UK. Increased frequencies were offered on all routes and air fares were lowered yet further. As a result, in 1995, by the time of the airline's tenth anniversary, Ryanair had become the biggest passenger carrier on the Dublin–London route, with total passengers of 2.25 million per annum and a work force of over 600 people.

1997 – A Milestone Year

The year 1997 marked a milestone for Ryanair. Thanks to the full EU air transport deregulation, the airline was free for the first time to open up new routes to continental Europe. Services were launched from London Stansted to Stockholm and Oslo, as well as from Dublin to Paris and Brussels. Again, Ryanair entering these markets offered air fares which were more than 50% lower than the cheapest fares then provided by the flag carrier airlines. Passengers responded enthusiastically and in great numbers to the arrival of low fares for the first time in these European markets. Ryanair was the first low fare airline to offer scheduled services from the UK to Continental Europe and *vice versa*. The same year, 1997, also saw Ryanair Holdings plc float on the Dublin and New York stock exchanges enabling all of its then 700 people to become shareholders in the airline. At the time the airline was capitalised at a market value of IR£300m, and was carrying over 3 million passengers per annum on its network of 18 routes. Ryanair was competing head to head with many of Europe's biggest airlines including British Airways, SAS, Alitalia, Lufthansa, Air France and Aer Lingus.

Continuing Growth

In 1999, Ryanair announced its next major investment programme with a US$2 billion order for up to 45 new Boeing 737–800 series aircraft. These are the latest and most modern aircraft manufactured by Boeing. The first five aircraft were delivered to Ryanair in 1999, and five more were scheduled for delivery each year thereafter. In 1999 Ryanair announced another set of record results, operating 35 routes to 11 countries, and carrying almost 6 million passengers. The company was then employing over 1200 people, and also had its shares listed on the London Stock Exchange as well as in

Dublin and New York (Nasdaq). In 1999, Ryanair was awarded 'Airline of the Year' by the Irish Air Transport Users Committee, and was voted one of the 'best managed' airlines in the world by the International Aviation Week magazine. In 2000, the airline launched its website at www.Ryanair.com, which within three months of its launch was taking over 50000 bookings per week by offering low air fares which started from as little as £1 return plus taxes on the Glasgow–London and £9 return plus taxes on the Dublin–London routes.

The airline continues to grow through the addition of extra routes and hubs carrying about 7 million passengers a year with hubs at Dublin and London (Stansted), and further hubs under development at Brussels (Charleoi) and Frankfurt (Hahn). The total network has grown to over 45 routes across 11 countries served with a fleet of 31 aircraft and 1400 people.

An Interview with Ryanair Chief Executive

[The interview with Micheal O'Leary reproduced below was conducted by Tom Chesshyre and appeared in the *Travel* section of *The Times* newspaper in January 2002.]

Michael O'Leary is late, just like so many of his aeroplanes. 'I'm terribly sorry,' gasps Ryanair's chief executive, as he rushes in 15 minutes after our scheduled appointment. 'You haven't been waiting long have you? Let me get you a tea. Or would you prefer coffee? Would you like a muffin; or something? No, are you sure? OK back in a couple of seconds.' And off he dashes to the counter of the Metro cafe at Stansted airport, hub for the airline's operation in the UK – looking apologetic and glancing over anxiously at me as he makes his order. All of which is making me feel just a little bit confused. You see, the *Times Travel* desk receives more complaints about Ryanair than any other airline – regarding everything from delays, to poor in-flight service, to damaged luggage, to lengthy check-in queues.

The Irish-based carrier, which has spearheaded the low-cost airline phenomenon in the past decade and which carried ten million passengers in the past year, crops up time and again in letters. A new complaint arrives virtually every week. Yet, as O'Leary is only too quick to point out, Ryanair rarely apologises or tries to make up for these problems. 'Are we going to say sorry for our lack of customer service?' he asks rhetorically, putting down his cheese and ham croissant (after offering part of it, most un-Ryanairishly, to me). 'Absolutely not. If a plane is cancelled will we put you up in a hotel overnight? Absolutely not. If a plane is delayed, will we give you a voucher for a restaurant? Absolutely not.'

But isn't this a bit harsh, I ask. Surely Ryanair and O'Leary – who has agreed to meet *Times Travel* to counter some of the complaints we have received about his airline – must care about customer service, to some extent? It can't just be a matter of saying 'tough luck' if a flight is delayed can it? Whatever happened to that old business maxim: the customer is always right? 'Listen,' he says bullishly. 'Our customer service is about the most well-defined in the world. We guarantee to give you the lowest airfare. You get a safe flight. You get a normally on-time flight. That's the package. We don't and won't give you anything more on top of that.' He pauses to take a sip of his tea – something passengers would have to pay for on board Ryanair flights. You even have to shell out for a packet of peanuts or a glass of mineral water. 'Listen, we care for our customers in the most fundamental way possible: we don't screw them every time we fly them.' (O'L eary, I soon realise, doesn't mince his words). 'We care for our customers by giving them the cheapest airfares. I have no time for certain large airlines which say they care and then screw you for six or seven hundred quid almost every time you fly.'

I'm getting the picture. But the fact is *Times Travel* still receives more complaints about Ryanair than any other airline. And many people are sick of the 'we've-got-the-cheapest-flights-so-grin-and-bear-it' approach – as the Air Transport Users' Council (AUC), which monitors airline complaints in the UK, testifies. The AUC says that Ryanair is one of the worst offending airlines; that it seems to 'stick two fingers up' at its disgruntled passengers; and that its delays record is poor for many European destinations. Recent findings from the Consumers' Association also show that fewer people would recommend Ryanair to a friend than any of the other main low-cost carriers: easyJet, buzz and Go. Isn't it time Ryanair moved on a bit and stopped thinking about customers as cattle to be transported frcm A to B? This sets off an O'Leary tirade, about the 'British Airways of this world', so I ask him about some of the specific complaints received from readers in recent weeks. For example, several have complained about how difficult it is to talk to anyone at the airline when they have a problem. Frustrated customers say they have to make endless phone calls before finally getting through to an operator. Doesn't this seem as though Ryanair is treating them with disdain?

'Our position is simple,' O'Leary says. 'Generally speaking, we won't take any phone calls because they keep you on the bloody phone all day. We employ four people in our customer care department,' he continues. 'I very complaint must be put in writing and we undertake to respond to that complaint within 24 hours. Anyway, do you know what 70 per cent of our complaints are about?' he says, sounding a bit aggrieved. 'They're about people who want to make changes to what are clearly stated as being "non-changeable, non-transferable and non-refundable" tickets.' He adopts a 'complaining' voice, mimicking a customer: 'I've changed my mind. My granny wasn't feeling well. I couldn't travel because I couldn't take time off work.' Aren't you being slightly cruel? 'No because even if you can't change your ticket and you've got to buy a second one, you're still going to save money compared with buying a single ticket from the major airlines. Anyway, with our new system you can make some changes. If you pay 20 euros (£12.30) you can change the time of your flight, but not the name on the ticket.' Which is a start.

Moving on to other reader gripes, I ask why Ryanair isn't more explicit about its use of secondary airports that are often miles from the destination that the airline headlines in its adverts. For example, Ryanair says it flies to Frankfurt, when it actually flies to Frankfurt's secondary airport, Hahn, 60 miles and a one-hour bus ride from Frankfurt City centre. Although it says so in the small print, surely the use of such airports should be made crystal clear to potential passengers? 'We'll be happy to do that some day, when other airlines describe Heathrow as being 35 miles outside London,' O'Leary says. 'This secondary airport matter is a typical one run up by the big airlines. They constantly say low-cost airlines take you to the middle of nowhere. It's what they said about Stansted ten years ago when we first flew here. They said: 'Oh, but Stansted's in Essex'. What? Like Heathrow's in Pall Mall or something?' But Hahn is still twice as far from the centre as Heathrow. And it doesn't have a 15-minute rail link. 'Look', O'Leary says. 'The more experienced traveller fundamentally wants to know: "Is that airport close to my destination?" If it's the main airport or not, that makes no difference to them.'

Regardless, many *Times* readers say they are frustrated at lead-in fares that are often unavailable. They say advertisements for £1 tickets encourage them to contact Ryanair, only to find that available tickets are much more expensive. The Advertising Standards Authority has upheld several complaints regarding fares headlined in Ryanair promotions. This really get: O'Leary going: 'When British Airways did its low-fares promotion it was only on a tiny percentage of sales,' he says. 'This compares with 75 per cent of our airfares that are sold in the two lowest categories. No other airline even comes close. And look what we did after September 11: instead of sitting aircraft on the ground, we carried more passengers. We gave out 300,000 seats for free. We sold a million seats for £9.99. That's caring, for you.'

Which brings us back to the whole question of customer service – and O'Leary's argument that low-cost airlines can get away with a no-frills service precisely because the fares themselves are low-cost. We don't seem to be getting anywhere. O'Leary says the proof of the pudding is that Ryanair attracts ten million passengers a year, a number of claims will treble by 2010 – more than BA. 'You can look at us in the most caustic light possible, that we're cheap Bush Paddies – but you can't get around the fact that people want to fly with us. In 16 months flying to Hahn airport, we've gone from nowhere to an 18 per cent market share.'

So how come we receive more complaints about Ryanair than easyJet, buzz and Go, its low-cost competitors? 'Just look at Frankfurt,' O'Leary says. 'That growth suggests to me that people really don't have much of a problem with us, do they?'

Sources

Tom Chesshyre, 'It's cheap but why not more cheerful?', *The Times, Travel Section*, Saturday 5 January, 2002. Reproduced with permission, ©Times Newspapers Limited 2002.
www. Ryanair.com.
UK Outbound Tour Operations.

CASE 6.6
THE UK OUTBOUND TOUR OPERATIONS INDUSTRY

The 'Package' Concept

Tourists travelling abroad can purchase each separate component of a holiday – accommodation, transportation, activities, ground handling, etc. – as individual items. During the 1960s, however, the foreign inclusive tour or 'package' holiday became established in Western Europe and brought with it a substantial expansion in the numbers of tourists venturing abroad.

A 'package' was defined by the European Commission in 1990 as a pre-arranged combination, sold or offered for sale at an inclusive price, of not less than two of the following three elements: transport; accommodation; and other tourist services not ancillary to transport or accommodation and accounting for a significant part of the package.

The role of the tour operators was the key element in the expansion of the package concept, which has continued to grow since it began in the 1950s. This role goes beyond that of the wholesaler, in that tour operators not only purchase or reserve the separate components in bulk but, in combining these components into an 'inclusive tour', they also become producers, since a new product, the inclusive tour or package holiday, is created. The traditional appeal of the tour operators' product has been to offer a complete holiday package at the lowest price to a population often lacking the linguistic knowledge or the knowledge and confidence to organise independent travel. As a result tour operation has become the dominant feature of the holiday market not only in the United Kingdom but also in most tourist-generaling countries.

Benefits of the Package Concept

Despite some industry commentators' comments over the years suggesting that the package holiday's days may be numbered (because many tourists have become more 'worldly-wise' and are prepared to travel independently), growth in the industry has been fuelled by three key selling points:

- the convenience of purchasing all the elements of the product in one purpose designed 'bundle';
- delivery of product quality assurance, reliability and protection;
- perceived good value prices.

But although the future of the 'package' seems assured, changes in consumer preferences and in the business environment are changing the characteristics of these packages, which will, in turn, have an effect on the future structure of this industrial sector. The tour operating sector as a whole (and the independent sector in particular), is facing a number of pressures which have led to a marked differences in recent performance.

The Growth of UK Outbound Tour Operations

Vladimar Raitz, a Russian émigré, is widely credited with operating the first Air Inclusive Tour (AIT) charter to Corsica in 1950, at an all-inclusive price of £32.10. Part of his original company, Horizon, continued until recent years as a trading name of Thomson. Others who pioneered AITs during the 1950s in the UK were Captain Ted Langton, who set up Universal Skytours (which was also later to become part of Thomson); Joe and Syril Shuman, founders of Global Holidays; Christopher and Stephen Lord whose Lord brothers firm was later absorbed by Laker Airways; George Jackman and Wilf Jones, who built up Cosmos; and Harry Chandler, whose family continues to control. The Travel Club of Upminster, founded in 1936.

Other companies missed out on the early market opportunities. Thomas Cook never achieved the market leadership in air holidays that it had in rail holidays, while British European Airways (BEA), a forerunner of British Airways, was slow to react to the threat posed by the charter airlines. In the 1950s foreign travel remained a luxury commodity within the reach of only a privileged few who had both plenty of free time and considerable purchasing power. The market changed during the 1960s, from that of a privileged 'niche' market to a 'mass' tourism market as a result of innovations in aircraft technology, changes in labour legislation (which provided for paid holidays in most European countries), and changes to the structure of the tour operating industry itself. Large companies had begun buying into tour operating as early as 1956 when Great Universal Stores acquired Global, but the industry remained highly fragmented during the 1950s and early 1960s.

The industry of the early 1960s was also beset by a number of company failures, including the failure in 1964 of Fiesta Tours, a major tour operator of the period. The Association of British Travel Agents (ABTA) had to step into rescue customers stranded abroad and in the aftermath calls were made for statutory controls of the burgeoning tour operating sector. ABTA responded from November 1966 with the introduction of the so-called 'Stabiliser Resolution'. Stabiliser was an attempt by ABTA to regulate the UK travel industry whereby ABTA member agents could sell only the foreign inclusive tours of ABTA tour operators, while ABTA tour operators could only sell through ABTA agents (or direct). It thus became impossible to build up a major market presence without belonging to ABTA. The Stabiliser Resolution did indeed help to stabilise the industry as the rate of failures fell after its introduction. Stabiliser remained in force until 1993 when ABTA relinquished the requirement upon the introduction of the EC directive on Package Travel, one effect of which was to require tour operators to provide financial protection to customers under law.

New Entrants and Consolidation

The strategic entry into the marketplace of the International Thomson Organisation (ITO) in 1965 proved to be a major turning point for the industry. It represented the initiation of a period of consolidation within the industry which continued until the late 1980s. The introduction of ITO meant the entry to the UK tour operations industry of a large, sophisticated and diversified international group of companies. During the summer of 1965 Thomson had around 100,000 holidays on offer. The Air Inclusive Tour (AIT) market (which is regulated in the UK by the Civil Aviation Authority (CAA) through the Air Travel Organisers' Licences (ATOLs) it issues each year) grew enormously during the period, but detailed figures are only available from 1976. Although many operators do not use their full ATOL allocation, the licences issued give an indication of the size of the total market and relative market shares.

The reasons for the rapid growth of the UK outbound AIT market and that of the operators are inextricably linked but perhaps two major factors stand out. First, many UK residents travel abroad for their holidays in order to obtain reliable sunshine and warmth. The UK's island location has necessitated the development of well-organised, packaged transportation to service this need. Second, UK residents accord holidays and travel a high priority in terms of their discretionary expenditure even in times of relative economic hardship.

Relatively low barriers to entry and continual striving among operators for increased market share led to price wars (particularly in the early 1970s and the mid- 1980s), which resulted in a highly volatile record of profitability over the period. The price wars, low margins and the vulnerability of the travel industry to external economic and political factors inevitably took their toll on operators. For example, Clarksons, which had expanded rapidly in the late 1960s, was losing money by 1971 and was taken over by the Court Line Group. The group had invested heavily in jet aircraft, but the 1973 oil crisis and economic recession led to the collapse of the company at the height of the summer season in August 1974. Parallels can be drawn between the International Leisure Group (ILG), which, when it failed in March 1991 was Britain's second largest tour operator, and Clarksons. The downturn in business at the time of the Gulf War exposed ILG's strategy of using strong tour operating cash flows to diversify into scheduled air services through its airline Air Europe.

During the 1970s and the 1980s the large tour operators came to increasingly dominate the AIT market, as mass market operators were determined to increase their market share and to reap the anticipated rewards of market dominance. Thomson, the market leader, had since its inception faced major challenges to its market leadership position, but had hitherto always successfully defended its position. Major competitors had disappeared from the scene: Clarksons collapsed in 1974; ILG collapsed in March 1991. Thomson's major challengers in the current marketplace are of more recent prominence. Owners Abroad (now renamed First Choice) was founded in 1972, and, as its name suggests, was a 'seat-only' specialist serving the needs of expatriate overseas property owners. Airtours started in 1978 as Pendle Airtours, a small operating division of David Crossland's travel agency Pendle Travel. The demise of ILG removed from the industry a privately held company that had targetted Thomson through aggressive pricing in a bid for an ever-greater share of the market. Both Airtours (since 1989) and First Choice are Public Limited Companies (PLCs). Their status as PLCs necessitated the targetting of profitability rather than market share as the primary objective of the two companies and as a result, competition since 1991 has focused on matching supply much more closely to demand, and thereby avoiding damaging price wars.

By 1990 a marked polarisation had occurred in the industry, dividing competitors into a relatively small number of 'mass' tour operators and a much larger number of 'independent' operators largely serving specialised niche markets. The term 'independent' tour operator has become widely used in the UK but it has no precise meaning. The term is often used loosely to describe any operator that is not one of the largest mass tour operators. One of the key features of independent tour operators is that they are not vertically integrated and they therefore rely on the supply in the marketplace for individual components of the package. With regard to the distribution of the products, the choice depends very much on the size of the organisation in terms of the number of passengers carried. Many of the small tour operators choose to apply direct sell methods. As one of the components of an air inclusive package is transport by air, the independents also need to secure capacity with either charter or scheduled airlines in order to assemble their products. In the UK the term 'independent' tour operator also has a more precise meaning, in that it can refer to those companies that are members of the Association of Independent Tour Operators (AITO). AITO was formed in 1976 in the wake of the Clarksons crash primarily to represent the views of smaller tour operators during the setting up of the CAA's bonding scheme. The association has grown to represent about 150 members that collectively carry some 1,500,000 customers per annum.

AITO members range from those carrying less than 500 customers per year to those carrying in excess of 100,000. The membership includes well-known companies that are part of the second tier of operators such as Balkan Holidays and Simply Travel, and less well-known names such as Sunvil Holidays. The membership also includes many tour operators that predominantly use car and ferries as means of transport. These companies, particularly a large number of French specialists, include well known names such as Eurocamp (which is a subsidiary of Holiday Break which has the status of a public limited company and carries over 250,000 customers a year), but do not appear in the ATOL listings, which solely cover AITs.

Competition, therefore, took place in two competitive arenas – the larger AITs competed with each other for the major 'volume' business whilst the independents, usually smaller companies, offered specialist products to niche markets. The temptation among the AITs to acquire within the independent sector was, however, limited by two factors: the constant threat of anti-monopoly legislation and a fear that the larger tour operators may be unable to 'think small' and flexible in a way that maintains quality for clients.

Clearly, given the scale and complexity of their operations, and the vertically and horizontally integrated structure of their businesses, the four largest operators in the UK can now be viewed as constituting a category of their own. Increasingly, however, given the size and international complexity of the companies concerned, it is apparent that a pan-European view of competition issues in the tour-operating sector will need to be taken in future. Expansion through integration does not only apply to the UK but the travel industry is also experiencing rapid internationalisation of ownership. If a company wants to be regarded as a major player in this sector it now needs to be part of a pan-European partnership, alliance or ownership structure of some sort. The aim of such international integration is to increase buying power abroad together with improvement of margins through airline fleet integration and combined ground handling.

The take-over of Thomson by its German rival Preussag during 2000, which required European Commission approval (that was granted during August 2000) is indicative of this trend. This purchase signalled a further round of merger and acquisition activity. C&N Touristic (Germany's second largest tour operator) gained control of Thomas Cook in December 2000 after Preussag had been forced to sell its controlling stake as a consequence of its purchase of Thomson.

Industry Features

Economies of Scale

One of the reasons often cited for ever-greater concentration by a few large suppliers of activities for an industry is that larger companies enjoy the advantages to be derived from economies of scale. These economies clearly exist in tour operating, in terms of marketing and purchasing economies for instance, but perhaps the influence of such economies is on the wane. The trend away from standard 'summer sun' packages towards a more diverse range of package options in the UK means that such economies of scale are harder to achieve. Tour operators are increasingly being forced to respond to a much more complex holiday market than has hitherto existed, through diversification, narrower market segmentation, catering for independently minded travellers and increasingly experienced customers. All of these trends reduce, to some extent, the advantages to be derived from economies of scale.

Furthermore, it is by no means clear that economies of scale are great beyond a certain size threshold in the industry. The increasing bureaucracy, expense of systems and the inflexibility of a larger scale of operations, can lead to diseconomies of scale resulting in higher not lower unit costs. The tour operating industry may well have many of the same characteristics as the airline industry. In the USA, the lowest cost 'producer' that other airlines seek to emulate is not one of the major carriers, but a medium sized airline called Southwest.

The four largest tour operating companies operating in the UK have become vertically (as well as horizontally integrated) in recent years, that is to say, that they own both inputs to the operating' process and control a part of the distribution channels for their products. To this end, the largest four tour operating brands of Thomson, Airtours, First Choice and JMC are part of groups which own airlines: Britannia, Airtours, Air 2000 and JMC respectively. The four companies also have extensive interests in travel agencies. Thomson, Airtours and JMC are part of groups which control the country's first, second and third largest travel agency chains: Lunn Poly, MyTravel (a re-branding of the former Going Places chain) and Thomas Cook respectively. First Choice, as well as owning the Travel Choice and Bakers Dolphin chains, has also developed a successful 'out of town' format with its Holiday Hypermarket concept which is spreading across the country.

The larger travel agency chains (which have themselves expanded their aggregate share of the total travel agency market), have increasingly favoured the larger operators that are able to offer bulk capacity and sufficient brochures to 'rack'. This trend has intensified as vertical integration has led to travel agencies favouring the operating brands of their owners, and operators seek preferential terms with agents. The tour operators have also developed direct forms of distribution through the development of dedicated call centres where staff are able to earn higher salaries than most travel agents if sales targets are met.

Regulatory Investigations

The increased concentration in the industry resulted in referral to the UK Mergers and Monopolies Commission (MMC – how known as the Competition Commission) on two occasions in 1989 and 1997. The MMC sought to investigate the issues arising out of possible anti-competitive behaviour by the largest tour operators in the UK. Later, in 2000, the European Commission investigated the UK industry in relation to the proposed takeover of First Choice plc by Airtours plc.

In 1989 the Thomson Travel Group was investigated for its takeover of Horizon plc as the industry worried that the long-term effects of the merger would cause the withdrawal of a number of operators from the industry, thereby increasing concentration and leading to adverse effects on price, choice, availability and standards of service. The takeover (of the UK's third largest tour operator of the time by its first) was allowed to proceed. The sector was investigated again in 1997 owing to the increase in the level of vertical integration by the larger tour operators. Smaller tour operators and travel agents again argued that this increase would bring about anti-competitive practices which would eventually squeeze them out of the market, leading to higher prices and less choice for consumers. However, in both investigations, the Commission found that the industry was broadly competitive and saw no significant reason to intervene, although in relation to vertical integration, recommendations were made in the 1997 report to:

- prevent tying discounts to the purchase of travel insurance;

- make travel agency ownership links more explicit;
- outlaw the practice of specifying discount levels to travel agencies by major operators.

The smaller tour operators were not only worried about the distribution of their products but also the supply of charter seats. In this regard the MMC concluded that, 'while there may be a shortage of capacity at weekends, there appears to be no shortage during the week'. One industry observer noted that the 1997 MMC investigation effectively gave a go-ahead for further consolidation in the industry.

Many of the smaller companies have successfully developed a niche in the market, usually by targetting particular customer types or by focusing on specific destinations. Furthermore, a number of niche operators have been acquired by the 'big four'. Innovative companies, which have created new products and discovered new destinations, have fallen to their more predatory competitors searching for greater economies of scale and scope. In doing so they have tried to combine the benefits of scale with the higher margins to be derived from the exploitation of successful niche markets. Nevertheless many middle-ranking operators remain vulnerable since, on the one hand, they fail to derive the benefits of scale, and on the other, they have failed to develop a niche market they can effectively defend. This vulnerability is likely to be greatest in the short-haul markets due to the structural characteristics of the industry. Concentration specifically in key short-haul markets is even higher than the figures indicated for overall concentration, a point that was to be emphasised by the European Commission investigation.

In November 1999 the European Commission prohibited a merger of two of the largest tour operators within the UK AIT market (Airtours and First Choice), on the grounds that the three largest operators effectively would control a large share of the short-haul market. The report stated that, 'the four large integrated suppliers already sell between them over 90% of all packages to mainland Spain, the Balearic Islands, the Canary Islands and Tunisia and 80% to [most] other significant short-haul summer destinations.' Concern was given in the report to the position of the remaining smaller tour operators since they would become further marginalised with regard to distribution, flight capacity and general competitiveness in the industry. The European Commission indicated that an excessively concentrated industry structure would emerge as a result of the proposed takeover. The potential removal of First Choice from the market would, the commission argued, remove the last remaining medium sized tour operator (and the only one with the potential to grow rapidly to the size of the three major suppliers). Finally, the takeover would have reduced competition at all three levels of the supply chain.

New Technologies

Tour operators in the UK have played an important part in the development of computerised bookings for tour packages. The investment in on-line interactive view data systems (during the 1970s and 1980s) resulted in the majority of the larger tour operators relying on this technology for most of their bookings. Other smaller operators have chosen not to automate and to rely instead on using conventional telephone calls as the main vehicle for bookings. This has worked to the advantage of the larger tour operators as travel agents have endeavoured to reduce telephone call charges and improve efficiency.

Foremost amongst the newer technologies is the development of Computerised Reservation Systems (CRS). CRS systems were first developed in the USA in the 1960s and 1970s as databases and booking systems for US airlines. They continued to develop and now include vast amounts of information on other transport providers, hotels, car hire provision, attractions and so on. Additionally, the reach of systems such as Amadeus and Galileo has expanded throughout the developed world as non-US airlines have forged partnerships with the US instigators of the systems.

In the USA 96% of travel agents are linked to a CRS system. CRS systems give travel agencies the ability flexibly to package exactly what the consumers want, thereby undermining the role of the traditional mass market tour operator. They can combine hotels, flights, car hire and so on using the CRS database. However, the role of the CRS in a British 'leisure traveller' context should not be overstated. There is a marked polarisation of business and leisure travel agencies with a low level of CRS penetration in the leisure travel agency sector. Many leisure travel agents are owned by tour operators which have invested heavily in their own view-data technology, and therefore have a vested interest in delaying the diffusion of CRS systems to the leisure travel agent sector.

Other technological development are also important. Distribution options include home shopping, point of sale multi-media booths, mail order and booking, particularly booking through the Internet.

The emerging tools of the Internet enable consumers to search on-line for information, to access reliable, accurate and up to date information, and quickly to compare comparative product offerings. Furthermore, the availability of such information enables consumers to make reservations in a fraction of the time necessary for some other methods and with a minimum of inconvenience. The Internet is driven by both the increasing volume and diversity of tourism demand and by the power it gives consumers to buy personalised 'bundles'of tourism products. In some cases this leads to the avoidance of the traditional tourism 'packages' leading instead to consumers assembling their own packages from individual component parts on offer.

Booking habits, however are slow to change, and use of the Internet for international travel requirements (other than flights) is comparatively small when compared to other forms of distribution – as at the year 2002 at least. Most Internet users, however, match the profile of the most desirable market segments in that they tend to be relatively well-educated professionals who travel frequently and have a higher disposable income. Furthermore, the Internet allows (at reasonable cost) suppliers an unprecedented opportunity to communicate globally with their target markets and to establish direct relationships with consumers.

Legal and Regulatory Developments

The EC Directive on Package Travel, Package Holidays and Package Tours was adopted on 13th June, 1990 and EU member states were required to implement its measures prior to 31st December, 1992. The main provisions of the directive are outlined below:

- *Article 2, Definitions* – The directive covers 'packages' which are defined as a pre-arranged combination of not less than two of three elements: transport; accommodation; and other tourist services.
- *Article 3, Descriptions and advertising* – The directive does not impose a legal obligation to provide a brochure, but where one is available it must contain in a legible, comprehensive and accurate manner both the price and adequate information concerning certain specified items such as the itinerary and the meal plan.
- *Article 4, The package travel contract* – Certain information is specified, such as information relating to passport and visa requirements, that the tour operator and/or the travel agent must provide to the consumer prior to travelling.
- *Article 5, Liability* – The tour operator becomes responsible for ensuring that all services under the package are rendered effectively and efficiently (whether rendered directly or by a third party).
- *Article 7, Financial security* – The tour operator must provide evidence of security for the refund of money paid over and for repatriation of the consumer in the event of insolvency.

The goal of the directive was to codify and harmonise existing EC legislation relating to package travel. In so doing much of the detailed implementation of the directive was left to the discretion of member states. In the UK, the Department of Trade and Industry took the view that it wanted to place a minimum of additional burdens on the sector and consequently opted for a self-regulating system.

As a result, 'bonding' in the UK is undertaken by a number of 'approved' schemes including those operated by ABTA, AITO, the Federation of Tour Operators (FTO) and the CAA. Under these systems a tour operator has to pay for a bond representing the value of an agreed proportion of their licensed capacity. The bond is forfeited in the event of failure to help reimburse customers. One effect of the implementation of the directive in the UK has been to include surface transport, and domestic packages as 'packages' requiring financial protection for the first time. The Directive, in requiring financial protection and greater scrutiny of activities, has raised the entry barriers to the tour operating sector in Europe, and forced some of the smaller, specialised tour operators to carry heavy additional financial burdens.

Changing Consumers

Mass tourism can be seen as a phenomenon of large-scale packaging of standardised leisure services at fixed prices for sale to a mass clientele. Clearly such tourism remains central to the outbound tourism product of the UK and several other north European countries, but underlying trends towards a new type of more independent and experienced traveller have been discerned.

These 'new tourists' have been described as consumers who are flexible, independent and experienced travellers, whose values and lifestyles are different from those of mass tourists. Six key attributes are characteristic of these 'new tourists.'

- *New consumers are more experienced* – In the UK the proportion of adults who had ever been on holiday abroad rose sharply from the 1960s through to the mid-1980s, reaching 67% in 1985. The figure has stayed close to this level ever since. In other words, first time buyers with sufficient income to enter the market had been captured and future growth (or decline) would reflect the motivations of experienced travellers. More experienced travellers are more knowledgeable and consequently more quality and value conscious, they demand greater choice and flexibility and are more certain of what they want and what they find unacceptable.

- *New consumers have changed values* – Values of conservation, health and nature are being reflected in the tour operators' products and there are growing signs that the fashion for the sun is beginning to fade.
- *New consumers have changed lifestyle* – One industry-watcher argued that society has moved through three key phases between the industrial era and today. First, from the industrial era in which people live to work to the post industrial era in which they worked to live, to the third phase where a new unity exists between work and leisure, and travel and leisure become integral aspects of daily life. These changes in the role of travel and leisure in society have implications for the travel industry. People who live to work have simple holiday and travel motivations while people who work to live view leisure as the counterpoint to everyday life. Those seeking unity of everyday life want to reduce the polarity between work and leisure and are looking for fulfilment throughout all sectors of life, during working time, through 'humanised' working conditions, and at home through more habitable cities and a more colourful everyday life.
- *New consumers are the products of changing population demographics* – Population demographics in the tourism generating countries are changing. In particular the population is ageing. These demographic changes will have profound effects upon buyer behaviour in tourist generating countries. It has been forecast that the early years of the twenty-first century will witness demographic shifts in Europe including a slight growth in the proportion of elderly people aged over 65, a large growth in the middle age categories and a relative decline in the 18 – 35 category. A significant European demographic trend was the rise of the 'baby boomers', that is those born between the Second World

Table 1
Motivations for Travel

People who live to work	*People who work to live*	*People seeking a unity between work and leisure*
to recover	to experience something different	to broaden their horizon
to recuperate	to explore	to learn something new
to rest	to have fun	to encourage introspection and communication with other people
to be served	to play	to discover the simple things in life and nature
to switch off	to be active	to foster creativity
	to relax without stress	to experiment
	to enjoy proximity to nature	to take personal risks
	to do as one pleases	

War and the mid-1960s, currently aged between their mid-30s and mid-50s. This category is inheriting wealth on a large scale leading to the higher net worth of middle-age households. They take wealth for granted, have higher expectations of the products and services that they buy and are likely to buy such products and services for their intrinsic qualities rather than for their status.

- *New consumers are more flexible* – Consumers are becoming 'hybrid' in nature in that they may consume in an unpredictable way, making the traditional stereotypical categories of rich, poor or middle income people no longer sufficient to segment holiday markets. Some consumers may, for instance, take the cheapest charter flight available but stay in the most luxurious accommodation available at the destination. Other consumers may stay in relatively modest accommodation but partake in expensive sporting activities such as heli-skiing or hot air ballooning. Another aspect of the flexible consumer is the spread of impulse buying to the travel industry. There are shorter lead times before booking and paying for holidays – a changing consumer preference which partially explains the growing number of shorter and more frequent breaks.

- *New consumers are more independent* – Consumers are increasingly asserting their individuality and independence, and seeking more flexible and custom-made travel and leisure options. They lend to resist the standardised and sanitised product options. This trend towards independence, individuality and more experimentation in travel and leisure is clearly underpinned by the value, lifestyle and demographic changes. Such changes are likely to manifest themselves in the continuing demand by consumers for the core advantages provided by packaged travel products relating to pricing, convenience, reliability and easy access. However, consumers are likely to increasingly reject some of the traditional drawbacks of packaged travel products relating to the inflexibility of products, and resistance to travelling in organised groups.

Appendix 6.6.1
Total ATOL Capacity

Year	*Total ATOL capacity (000s)*	*Year*	*Total ATOL capacity (000s)*
1976	8345	1989	13982
1977	7424	1990	13065
1978	8578	1991	10061
1979	5303	1992	14920
1980	6164	1993	15468
1981	6661	1994	18539
1982	7067	1995	22723
1983	7938	1996	22951
1984	8623	1997	24980
1985	8647	1998	27926
1986	9843	1999	27942
1987	12598	2000	30652
1988	14567	2001	32470

Source: CAA, various.

Appendix 6.6.2
Largest Tour Operators Licensed Capacity

Year	*5 largest tour operators' market share (ooos)*	*Tour operators in order of market share*
1976	1553	Thomson, Cosmos, Silverwing, Laker Air, Horizon-Midlands
1977	1502	Thomson, Cosmos, Silverwing, Horizon-Midlands, Laker Air
1978	1521	Thomson, Cosmos, Silverwing, Horizon-Midlands, Laker Air
1979	1875	Thomson, Silverwing, Cosmos, Horizon, Laker Air
1980	2165	Thomson, Silverwing, Horizon, Cosmos, Owners Services
1981	2263	Thomson, Silverwing, Horizon, Cosmos, Owners Services
1982	2913	Thomson, Silverwing, Intasun, Horizon, Cosmos
1983	3142	Thomson, British Airways, Intasun, Horizon, Rank
1984	3076	Thomson, Horizon, Intasun, British Airways Rank
1985	3456	Thomson, Horizon, Intasun, Rank, British Airways
1986	5041	Thomson, Horizon, Intasun, Rank, British Airways
1987	8493	Thomson, ILG, Horizon, British Airways, First Choice
1988	8985	Thomson, ILG, Horizon, Redwing, First Choice
1989	10022	Thomson, ILG, First Choice, Redwing, Airtours
1990	8899	Thomson, ILG, First Choice, Airtours, Yugotours
1991	6088	Thomson, First Choice, Airtours, Yugotours, Sunworld
1992	8353	Thomson, First Choice, Airtours, Cosmos, Sunworld
1993	8600	Thomson, First Choice, Airtours, Cosmos, Sunworld
1994	10719	Thomson, Airtours, First Choice, Cosmos, Sunworld

Year	*5 largest tour operators' market share (ooos)*	*Tour operators in order of market share*
1995	11799	Thomson, Airtours, First Choice, Cosmos, Sunworld
1996	10253	Thomson, Airtours, First Choice, Cosmos, Unijet
1997	11952	Thomson, Airtours, First Choice, Thomas Cook, Cosmos
1998	16009	Thomson, Airtours, First Choice, Thomas Cook, Carlson
1999	15921	Thomson, Airtours, Thomas Cook, First Choice, Cosmos
2000	18218	Airtours, Thomson, Thomas Cook, First Choice, Cosmos
2001	18518	Airtours, Thomson, Thomas Cook, First Choice, Cosmos

Note: Tour operator figures are for the group of companies, where an operator has more than one operating brand.
Source: CAA, various.

Since 1990 the Civil Aviation Authority (CAA) has published data on the actual carryings of the total AIT market and from 1991 this data has been broken down to itemize the actual carryings of individual ATOL holders. The CAA data on actual carryings can be categorised in order to distinguish between two groupings of tour operators:

- *First tier operators* – consisting of the largest five tour operators.
- *Other operators* – which include all remaining actual carryings by ATOL holders.

Following the introduction of new ATOL regulations in May 1995, three kinds of business are specified in licences. These are:

- *'Fully Bonded'* – scheduled or charter based inclusive packages and seat-only travel on charter flights (1406 licences December 1996).

Appendix 6.6.3
Largest Tour Operators' Capacity

Tour Operator	*1990 ATOL capacity (000s)*	*1991* ATOL capacity (000s)*	*1992 ATOL capacity (000s)*	*1993 ATOL capacity (000s)*	*1994 ATOL capacity (000s)*	*1995 ATOL capacity (000s)*	*1996 ATOL capacity (000s)*	*1997 ATOL capacity (000s)*	*1998 ATOL capacity (000s)*	*1999 ATOL capacity (000s)*	*2000 ATOL capacity (000s)*	*2001 ATOL capacity (000s)*
Thomson	4348	3015	3326	3488	3801	4281	4032	4440	5080	5080	4725	4568
ILG	1798	a										
First Choice	798	1621	2275	1939	2042	2373	2029	1917	3164	3068	3210	3557
Airtours	635	828	1488	1692	2438	2946	2671	3083	3841	3930	5330	5540
Cosmos	b	b	822	1081	1805	1453	831	1049	b	1132	1294	1269
Yugotours	320	340	b	f								
Sunworld[d]/T. Cook	b	284	442	400	633	746	b	1463	2711	2711	3659	3584
Unijet	b	b	b	b	b	b	690	b	e	e		
Carlson	b	b	b	b	b	b	b	b	1213	g		
Total Largest five	8899	6088	8353	8600	10719	11799	10253	11952	16009	15921	18218	18518
Total All tour operators	13065	10061	13575	14545	17136	18813	21995	19819	22231	23264	24039	25362

Notes:
a ILG was placed in receivership in March 1991.
b Not placed in the top five tour operators.
c Airtours' 1994 and 1995 figures include Aspro which was acquired in June 1993.
d Became Thomas Cook after 1997.
e Part of First Choice after 1997.
f Ceased trading.
g Traded as part of Thomas Cook from 1999.
* Gulf War.
Source: CAA, various.

Appendix 6.6.4
Actual Carryings

Tour Operator	*1991 carry-ings (000s)*	*1992 carry-ings (000s)*	*1993 carry-ings (000s)*	*1994 carry-ings (000s)*	*1995 carry-ings (000s)*	*1996 carry-ings (000s)*	*1997 carry-ings (000s)*	*1998 carry-ings (000s)*	*1999 carry-ings (000s)*	*2000 carry-ings (000s)*	*2001 carry-ings (000s)*
Thomson	2850	3247	3481	3950	4208	3657	3917	4679	4869	4037	3917
First Choice	1658	2094	1878	1915	1928	1992	1875	2919	2973	2844	2949
Airtours	993	1437	2135	2427	2720	2488	2877	3618	3961	4338	5087
Cosmos	600	864	1135	1562	1091	931	965	957	991	1084	1134
Sunworld/T. Cook	239	461	429	661	705	a	1050	2352	2901	3232	3292
Unijet	a	a	a	a	a	649	b				
First tier Sub-total	6340	8103	9058	10515	10652	9717	10684	14525	15695	15535	16379
Other	4040	4807	5192	6085	7648	10983	11416	9975	10605	11965	12821
Total	10380	12910	14250	16600	18300	20700	22100	24500	26300	27500	29200

Notes:
Figures relate to all licences for 12-month periods to the end of September.
[a] Not placed in the top five tour operators.
[b] Part of Thomas Cook.
Source: CAA, various.

- *'Lower Bonded'* – scheduled seat-only tickets covered by a bond. These are bonded at a lower level than packages and charters, usually, 5% (186 licences December 1996).
- *'Agency'* – scheduled seat-only tickets where an airline guarantees the business of a consolidator and provides a 'Deed of Undertaking' to the CAA (63 licences December 1996).

The introduction of Lower Bonded and Agency ATOLs from 1995 accounts for a large (although not precisely quantifiable) part of the increase in ATOL capacity between 1995 and 1996.

Appendix 6.6.5
Number of ATOL Holders

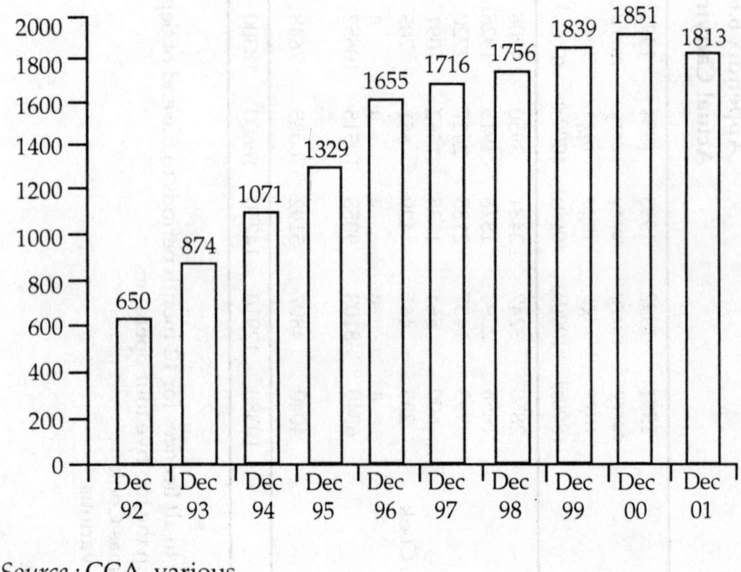

Source : CCA, various.

Appendix 6.6.6
Average Prices, Total Revenue and Retail Price Indices

	1992	*1993*	*1994*	*1995*	*1996*	*1997*	*1998*	*1999*	*2000*	*2001*
Average holiday price	£318	£346	£356	£361	£388	£415	£415	£421	£438	£447
Total revenue (£bn)	4.1	4.9	5.9	6.6	7.8	9.2	10.2	11.0	12.0	13.1
Retail price index (1987 = 100)	138.5	140.7	144.1	149.1	152.7	157.5	162.9	165.4	170.3	173.3

Note: Table shows actual average prices charged by tour operators for 12 months to September.
Source: CAA, various.

Sources

D. Buhalis (2001) The tourism phenomenon: the new tourist and consumer, in S. Wahab and C. Cooper (eds), *Tourism in the Age of Globalisation*, Routledge, London.

Civil Aviation Authority, *ATOL Business*, Civil Aviation Authority, London, 1992 – 2001.

European Commission, *Council Directive of June 13, 1990 on Package Travel*, Package Holidays and Package Tours (90/314/EEC).

J. Krippendorf (1986) Tourism in the system of industrial society, *Annals of Tourism Research;* 13(4).

J. Krippendorf (1987) *The Holidaymakers; understanding the Impact of Leisure and Travel*, London, Heinemann.

Victor T.C. Middleton (1991) Whither the package tour? *Tourism Management*, September.

Auliana Poon (1993) *Tourism Technology and Competitive Strategies*, Wallingford, CABI.

Chris Ryan (1991) UK package holiday industry, *Tourism Management*, March 1991.

C. Smith and P. Jenner (1998) Travel agents in Europe, *Travel and Tourism Analyst*, 4, 5 – 15.

TTG (1998) The year that shook the travel world, *Travel Trade Gazette*, 6 January.

7

STRATEGIC METHODS OF DEVELOPMENT FOR TRAVEL AND TOURISM

INTRODUCTION

The decision as to which method of strategic development to adopt is critical to the success of strategy. The variety of methods used for development will be considered, together with a critical appraisal of the success or failure of these methods.

The chapter briefly considers internal (or organic) growth, and then discusses the various mechanisms of external development. The recent trend in collaborative arrangements such as the strategic alliance is discussed and finally, the chapter looks at 'downsizing' strategies such as demerger.

LEARNING OBJECTIVES

After studying this chapter, students should be able to:

- define and distinguish between internal and external business growth;
- describe the various types of merger and acquisition;
- explain the motivations behind mergers and acquisitions and the reasons why they succeed or fail;
- describe what is meant by the various forms of joint development such as strategic alliances, and why organisations enter into them;

- explain what is meant by a disposal and describe why organisations pursue this pathway;
- understand the regulatory and legal frameworks that influence business growth.

Alternative Strategic Methods

Having considered the direction of development and aspects of competitive strategy we can now turn to a consideration of the strategic methods that can be employed to achieve the strategic objectives that have been set. In determining the methods by which strategic development will take place the management of a travel and tourism organisation is faced with making a choice between three basic options:

- to develop internally (or organically as it is sometimes called), utilising existing available resources;
- to merge with or acquire other companies, or;
- to develop some form of joint development with other organisations by making some form of collaborative arrangement.

Clearly many organisations use each of the alternative strategic options in different circumstances. The same company may, for instance, choose to grow organically in one market, acquiring another company in a second market and form a collaborative venture in a third market in recognition of the differing market characteristics that exist.

Organic (Internal) Growth

The Commonest Mechanism of Growth

Organic growth is the most straightforward mechanism of business growth. Most companies have used internal growth as their main method of growth at some time, and so its 'popularity' is obvious. The essential feature of organic growth is the reinvestment of previous years' profits in the existing business, together with finance provided by shareholders and banks. By increasing capacity (by, say, offering a larger number of holidays for sale), the organisation takes on more employees to cope with the extra demand. In so doing, turnover increases and so does the capital (balance sheet) value of the business.

Organic growth is common during the early stages of corporate development as companies build markets and develop new products. However, large companies may use it alongside external growth to consolidate market position. The introduction of an additional cruise ship by a cruise line is an example of internal growth. Earlier years retained profits, possibly enhanced by additional funding provided by banks or shareholders, are channelled into the development and the organisation benefits from the increased market share and increased turnover.

Organic growth offers a number of potential advantages over other methods of development:

- It is usually a lower risk option, in that the increase in capacity remains fully under the control of the existing management thereby avoiding the risks of dealing with other organisations.
- Core competences can usually be exploited and existing expertise can be capitalised upon.
- The problems associated with the integration of differing organisational cultures are avoided.
- Disruption of cash flows is likely to be less than in the case of mergers or acquisitions and to a lesser extent with the various forms of joint development.

On the other hand, organic growth is also associated with a number of potential disadvantages:

- It is usually a slower mechanism compared to the external growth methods where the 'bolting on' of a new company or cooperation with other organisations is a faster route to growth than gradual growth by internal means.
- Relying on the competences and resources of a single organisation may lead to shortages and might mean that important opportunities are not exploited.

Many large companies have used this method extensively in reaching their present size, but few have used the method exclusively. Thus, when British Airways developed a low cost subsidiary airline ('Go Airlines') in the late 1990s, the airline chose to develop the airline internally from scratch rather than purchase an existing low cost airline, such as perhaps Ryanair or easyJet, or to collaborate in the development with an existing airline. Similarly, the Marriott hotel corporation developed its Courtyard hotels concept organically during the 1990s, from the drawing board through to its current international market penetration in major business cities (Crawford-Welch, 1994).

This method tends to be chosen in circumstances where:

- suitable partners for joint development are unavailable;
- merger or acquisition is prevented on the grounds of cost, unavailability of suitable targets or regulatory disapproval;
- directors want to maintain control;
- the necessary resources and competences are available internally.

Internal growth is expansion by means of the reinvestment of previous years' profits, loan and share capital in the existing business. This results in increased capacity, increased employment and ultimately, increased turnover.

- *Advantages* – lower risk, within existing area of expertise, avoids high exposure to costs of alternative growth mechanisms (e.g. by debt servicing).
- *Disadvantages* – slower than external growth, little scope for diversification, relies upon the skills of existing management in the business.

External Mechanisms of Growth – Mergers and Acquisitions (M&As)

Definitions

It is difficult to open the business press without encountering details of a proposed or progressing merger or acquisition. The term *merger* is however sometimes replaced in such text with the word *takeover* or by *acquisition*. The same news story may use all three terms as though the words meant the same thing. For the purposes of a strategy text such as this, it is important to clarify the main terms generally used in connection with this process.

In a *merger* the shareholders of the organisations come together, normally willingly, to share the resources of the enlarged (merged) organisation, with shareholders from both sides of the merger becoming shareholders in the new organisation.

For example, in November 2001, in the business downturn following the September 2001 terrorist attacks on the USA, P&O Princess Cruises and the Royal Caribbean cruise line announced plans to merge. The merger, which was announced as a 'merger of equals', would form the world's largest cruise company with 41 ships offering 75000 berths. The top jobs would be shared between managers of the two companies and the merger it was stated would lead to the saving of US dollars 100 million in annual operating economies.

An *acquisition* is a 'marriage' of unequal partners with one organisation buying and subsuming the other party. In such a transaction the shareholders of the target organisation cease to be owners of the enlarged organisation unless payment to the shareholders is paid partly in shares in the acquiring company. The shares in the smaller company are bought by the larger.

For example, over the past few years the leading UK outbound tour operators have been very active in acquiring smaller rivals. The leading tour operator, the Thomson Travel Group, for example acquired tour operators such as Austravel, Crystal Holidays and Tropical Places in the late 1990s. However, Thomson was itself acquired during 2000 by Preussag (now renamed Tui) a leading German industrial conglomerate based in Hanover, which included tour operating, airlines and travel distribution in its portfolio of activities under brand names such as TUI, Hapag-Lloyd and Fritidsresor.

A *takeover* is technically the same as an acquisition, but the term is often taken to mean that the approach of the larger acquiring company is unwelcome from the point of view of the smaller target company. The term *hostile takeover* describes an offer for the shares of a target public limited company which the target's directors reject. If the shareholders accept the offer (despite the recommendation of the directors) then the hostile takeover goes ahead.

For example, an attempted takeover of First Choice plc by Airtours plc (now renamed MyTravel plc), which would have involved the takeover of the UK's third largest integrated travel business by the second, was resisted by the board of First Choice and was eventually blocked after intervention by the European Commission in 1999. A further example is provided by an acrimonious battle in the cruise sector. In 2000 Carnival Corporation of the USA, the world's largest cruising company, and Star Lines, the world's fourth largest cruise line which is based in Hong Kong, both tried to takeover the Norwegian Cruise Line based in Miami. After an expensive and hard fought battle Star Lines succeeded in wresting control of the takeover target.

Whichever of these routes is taken, the result is a larger and more financially powerful company. The world *integration* is the collective term used to describe these growth mechanisms.

A Brief History of M&As

All public limited companies have a market value. Market value equals the number of shares on the stock market (the *share volume*) multiplied by the share price. It is taken to be a good indicator of the value of a company because it accounts for the company's asset value plus the 'goodwill' that the market attaches to the shares. It follows that the combined market value of a merger or acquisition is the two companies' values added together. It is an indication of what the company will be valued at after the integration goes ahead.

Whilst the M&A process is a well-used mechanism in strategic development, recent history has shown that UK based companies have used it rather more than those based in mainland Europe. Only in the USA have companies used the mechanism to a similar extent. However, recent figures show increased merger and acquisition activity in the global economy generally as companies feel the need to increase in size to become more internationally competitive.

One of the consequences of M&A activity is that many of the well-known 'names' of yesteryear have disappeared while some of today's best-known companies are relatively young in their current form: examples are C&N Touristik (now renamed Thomas Cook AG) owned jointly by Lufthansa, the German airline, and Karstadt, a leading German department store group, operated Condor a large charter airline and a large tour operation operating several brands including Neckermann. In December 2000 the company completed the acquisition from Preussag (another German company) of Thomas Cook, the well-known travel and travellers cheque brand which is usually credited with having been the world's first tour operator, having started operations in the UK during the 1840s.

A common misunderstanding surrounding the integration process is that two organisations always come together in their entirety. In practice, many integrations are the result of one organisation joining with a divested *part* of another. That is to say that one company has made a strategic decision to withdraw from an industry or market and in an attempt to maximise the value of the resources it no longer wants (i.e. an unwanted part of the previous company structure), it sells them to another company. The reasons why companies demerge and sell subsidiaries in non-core elements is addressed later in this chapter.

Explanations and Motivations for M&As

There are a number of potential reasons for pursuing an external growth strategy. We have already encountered the overall objective of growth, but growth is seldom a stand-alone objective. The question is *why is growth a desired objective?* The following is a summary of these motivations.

- To *increase market share* in order to increase pricing power in an industry.
- To *enter a new market*, possibly to offset the effects of decline in current markets or to broaden market portfolio.
- To *reduce competition*, possibly by purchasing a competitor.
- To *gain control of valuable brand names* or pieces of intellectual property like patents.
- To gain preferential *access to distribution channels* (to gain factor inputs on preferential terms or to secure important supplies) by purchasing a supplier.
- To *broaden product range* in order to exploit more market opportunities and to spread risk.
- To *develop new products* for the market faster than internal research and development could do.
- To *gain access to new production or information technologies* in order to reduce costs, increase quality or increase product differentiation.
- To *gain economies of scale*, such as by increasing purchasing power so that inputs can be purchased at lower unit cost.
- To *make productive use of spare or underused resources*, such as finance that is sitting on deposit in a bank.
- To *'asset strip'* – the practice of breaking up an acquired company and recovering more than the price paid by selling the parts separately.

- To *enhance corporate reputation* (appropriate if the existing company name has been associated with an alleged misdemeanour).

The precise nature of the integration selected will depend upon the specific objectives being pursued. If, for example, market share is the most important objective, then it is likely that a company will seek a suitable horizontal integration. On the other hand, a vertical integration would be more appropriate if supply or distribution concerns are uppermost amongst a company's threats.

External growth is usually expensive and it therefore has significant financial resource implications, not to mention sizeable bills presented by lawyers and merchant (investment) bankers who are inevitably brought into advise on the process. Accordingly, it is entered into for specific strategic purposes that cannot be served through the normal progression of organic development.

Synergy – The Main Objective of M&As

Overriding all other purposes served by integration is that of synergy. Synergy refers to the benefits that can be gained when organisations join forces rather than work apart. An integration can be said to be synergistic when the *whole is greater than the sum of the parts.* More popularly, synergy can be expressed as '2 + 2 = 5.' If the integration is to achieve synergy, the 'new' company must perform more efficiently than either of the two parties would have done had they remained separate.

On a simple level, we can conceptualise synergy using a human example. When two people work *together* performing a task like lifting heavy logs onto a lorry, they can achieve far more work than two people lifting logs separately. A rally team of two enables the team to win a race if they work together with one driving and one navigating. If the two were to work separately, then each person would have to drive and navigate at the same time.

Synergy is measured in terms of increased added value. Kay (1993) made the point that, 'Value is added, and only added [in an integration] if distinctive capabilities or strategic assets are exploited more effectively. A merger adds no value if all that is acquired is a distinctive capability which is already fully exploited, as the price paid will reflect the competitive advantage held.' Accordingly, integrations that do not enable the 'new' organisation to produce higher profits or consolidate a stronger market position are usually deemed to have been relatively unsuccessful. The next section describes why failures sometimes occur.

Potential Problems with M&A – Why do they Sometimes go Wrong?

The fact that mergers and acquisitions are undoubtedly popular as methods of business growth may lead us to conclude that they are always successful. In practice, this is not always true. A number of studies have analysed the performance of companies after integrations and the findings are not very encouraging (see for example Kay, 1995, Porter, 1985; Ravenscraft and Scherer, 1987).

These studies found that many corporate 'marriages' failed to work and ended in divorce. Of those that did survive, Kay (1995) found that when profitability before and after the integration were compared, a 'nil to negative effect' was achieved.

The main failure factors

There are a number of reasons why integrations do not work. We can summarise these 'failure factors' under six headings.

1. *Lack of research* into the circumstances of the target company (and hence incomplete knowledge). Failure in this regard can result in some nasty surprises after the integration.

2. *Cultural incompatibility* between the two parties.
3. *Lack of communication* within and between the two parties.
4. *Loss of key personnel* in the target company after the integration.
5. *Paying too much for the acquired company* and hence overexposing the acquiring company to financial risk.
6. *Assuming that growth in a target company's market will continue indefinitely.* Market trends can fall as well as rise.

Government Policy and Integrations

Government policy on mergers may have contributed to some integration failures. Corporate growth can be restricted by government (which in the UK is represented by the Competition Commission, formerly the Monopolies and Mergers Commission), as companies are only allowed to establish a certain market share. In the UK an integration which would result in the new organisation controlling over 25% of the market is generally subject to government scrutiny which often results in such a merger being blocked. Being prevented from expanding in a related area may force some companies to take the more risky route of diversification (acquiring a company making different products in different markets).

Success Factors for M&A

History has shown that mergers and acquisitions work best when the initiator company follows a number of intuitively obvious 'rules'. They are designed to offset the failure factors we identified above. The chances of success might be increased by:

- The *identification of a suitable 'target' candidate* with whom to merge or acquire. The emphasis on the word *suitable* is expanded upon below.
- A preparation for an approach should involve a detailed evaluation of the target company's *competitive*

position. This would typically comprise a survey of its profitability, its market share, its product portfolio, its competitiveness in resource markets and so on.

- Consideration being given to the *competibility of the two companies' management styles and culture*. Because integrations often involve the merging of the two boards of directors, it is usually important that the directors from the two companies are able to work together. In addition, the cultures, if not identical in character, should be able to be brought together successfully.
- The possibility of a successful marriage between the two *corporate structures*. If one is, for example, very tall and centralised and the other is shorter and decentralised, problems may occur in attempting to bring the two together.
- Retaining key personnel. If the target company has key personnel (say a key manager or a distinctive research capability resident within a number of uniquely qualified scientists), then measures should be taken to ensure that these *key people are retained after the integration*. This can often be achieved by holding contractual talks with these people before the integration goes ahead.
- The initiating company ensuring that the *price paid for the target* (of the valuation of its shares) *is realistic*. A key calculation of any investment is the return made on it and this is usually measured as the profit before interest and tax divided by the price paid for it. It follows that the return on investment (as a percentage) will depend upon the price paid for the target company. The valuation of a company is a complex accounting calculation, which depends the balance sheet value, the prospects and performance of the company, and the value of its intangible assets (such as its brands, patents, etc.)

Accordingly, the importance of detailed information-gathering before the integration cannot be overemphasised.

External Growth without M&A – Joint Development

A joint development is where two or more organisations share resources and activities to pursue a strategy (Johnson and Scholes, 2002). The development method has been increasingly popular over recent years as organisations seek help and support from other organisations. Increasingly complex environments (such as globalisation) has meant that organisations often cannot cope through using their own resources and competences alone. Joint developments enable organisations to avoid some of the limitations of mergers and acquisitions, such as regulatory restrictions, whilst still gaining the benefits of collaboration.

Collaborative strategy (or cooperative strategy as it is often termed) is rapidly becoming the counterpart to competitive strategy as a key strategic management tool (Faulkner and Bowman, 1995). In rapidly globalising world markets, collaborative strategy is the engine driving companies that are deficient in certain competences, resources or assets, to link together with other companies in a similar predicament in order to drive jointly the competitive advantages they lack on their own. As Ohmae (1989) observed in comparing commercial organisations with the foreign policies of national governments, 'companies are just beginning to learn what nations have always known: in a complex, uncertain world filled with dangerous opponents, it is best not to go it alone'.

In categorising these collaborative agreements theoretical bases have been advanced. Contractor and Lorange (1988), for instance, viewed interorganisational collaboration in terms of the degree of interdependency between the parties involved. Faulkner (1995) categorised collaborative relationships in relation to their degree of integration ranging from markets to hierarchies, with the market end of the spectrum being dominated by the price mechanism and the hierarchy being dominated by organisational decisions. Between the two extremes a range of interorganisational

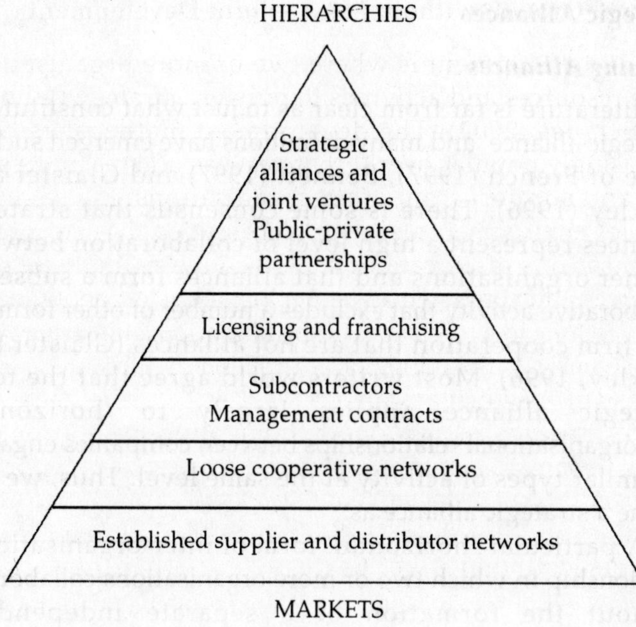

Figure 7.1: The intermediate organisational forms between markets and hierarchies.

forms exist with ascending levels of integration. Strategic alliances and joint ventures represent the most integrated form of interorganisational collaboration. Further integration represents a single corporate form subject to fully integrated decision-making. Figures 7.1 illustrates Faulkner's categorisation of interorganisational forms.

Here we will focus on those aspects of joint development of most relevance to travel and tourism namely:

- Strategic alliances and joint ventures
- Public-private partnerships
- Franchising
- Management contracts
- Cooperative networks.

Strategic Alliances

Defining Alliances

The literature is far from clear as to just what constitutes a 'strategic alliance' and many definitions have emerged such as those of French (1997), Bennett (1997) and Glaister and Buckley (1996). There is some consensus that strategic alliances represent a high level of collaboration between partner organisations and that alliances form a subset of collaborative activity that excludes a number of other forms of interfirm cooperation that are not alliances (Glaister and Buckley, 1996). Most writers world agree that the term strategic alliance applies largely to 'horizontal' interorganisational relationships between companies engaged in similar types of activity at the same level. Thus, we can define a strategic alliance as:

A particular 'horizontal' form of inter-organisational relationship in which two or more organisations collaborate, without the formation of a separate independent organisation, in order to achieve one or more common strategic objectives.

Bennett (1997) distinguished between 'tactical' alliances, which are loose forms of collaboration that exist to gain marketing benefits and 'strategic' alliances which are characterised by being longer, and wider in their scope and level of commitment. A strategic alliance also involves, in many cases, a demonstration of commitment by way of *equity swaps* in which the partner companies purchase minority equity stakes in each other thereby having a vested interest in ensuring the financial success of partners. In categorising strategic alliances, most writers would exclude buyer-seller relationships, subcontracting, franchising, and licensing, where to some degree the parties involved may have opposing goals and the relationships are 'vertical' between organisations along the channel of distribution.

The distinction between *joint ventures* and *strategic alliances* is one of emphasis rather than fundamental distinguishing characteristics. A joint venture normally implies joint ownership of assets by the parties involved, the formation of separate independent operating companies for the management of the shared activities, and collaboration on a relatively narrow range of activities. In practice the distinction between the two terms is often blurred.

The major Global Distribution Systems (GDS) operating in the travel industry (such as Sabre and Galileo) would be termed joint ventures since separate independent operating entities have been formed by the collaborating airlines and other investors which own these systems. These companies operate in a relatively autonomous fashion having their own offices, infrastructure and access to capital. Illinois based Galileo, for instance, was floated on the New York stock exchange in 1997. As a British Airways spokesman stated on the sale of the company's remaining 6.7% stake in the GDS in June 1999, 'Galileo is in a non-core area for us.' By way of contrast, strategic alliances have been formed between some airlines and these have been at the heart of the strategic development for the airlines involved. Although there have been some cross-equity holdings, most participants' core assets are directly owned and managed by the constituent airlines. Furthermore, the organisations established to manage the alliances are subject to the direct involvement of the airline alliance partners involved, only having minor devolved responsibilities.

Strategic Alliances in the Travel Industry

The formation of strategic alliances has been evident in many industries including pharmaceuticals, vehicle manufacture and chemicals, and this process has been replicated in the international travel industry where alliances have come to form a central feature of the developing industrial structure. Alliances have been growing between airline and accommodation companies (with ancillary services such as car rental often also involved). It is clear that collaborative arrangements of various types have become an increasingly important strategic method of development in the travel industry, although statistical data indicating success or otherwise is often lacking. Many writers, including Gialloreto (1989), Dev *et al.* (1996), Granham (1996), Alamadari and Morell (1997), Bennett (1997), French (1997) and Oum and Park (1997), have pointed to the high level of activity in the field of travel industry alliance formation.

However, the alliances differ in:

- their motives;
- their scope;
- their structures;
- their objectives;
- the ways in which they are managed.

The motivations for forming strategic alliances in the travel industry are numerous and complex, and a full discussion of these motivations is beyond the scope of this chapter. It is clear, however, that the recent economic history of the international travel industry has been characterised by the emergence of many alliances, some of which have subsequently failed and new realignments of companies have been forged. Long-standing 'natural' alliances between travel companies and accommodation providers which saw the ownership of hotels by railway, shipping and airline companies, have been replaced by other arrangements as inter-company and inter-modal competition has increased (Garnham, 1996). Throughout the 1980s, alliance formation in the global travel industry increased until the position was reached in the early 1990s at which most of the world's major airline, hotel and car rental firms were linked by a web of cross-shareholdings, joint ventures, and joint sales and service arrangements (Dev *et al.*, 1996).

Many examples of a liances exist in the airline and hotel sectors, although many fall short of being 'strategic' in the true sense. Some are probably best described as 'tactical' in their orientation, focusing primarily on marketing and information technology collaboration, rather than wider collaboration. In distinguishing between three levels of alliance on the basis of short-term, medium-term or long-term (strategic) relationships, Dev and Klein (1993) argued that in such a hierarchy of relationships, partners often progress from the simple short-term relationships through to complex strategic relationships, but that only at the strategic level do alliances offer companies the ability to respond to the pressures of global competition and illiquidity. Potential benefits, they argued, accrue from enhanced market coverage both geographically and by segment; greater economies of scale in advertising, sales, distribution and purchasing; and complementary strengths in operations and marketing.

Strategic Alliances – Examples from the Hotel and Tour Operating Sectors

Radisson Hotels, part of the Carison group of travel companies, has expanded through an international strategy based on strategic alliances with local hotel groups around the world such as Edwardian Hotels in the UK and Movenpick based in Switzerland (Olsen, 1993). Hilton Hotels also provide a case study illustrating the benefits to be derived from a collaborative approach. The two arms of Hilton, Hilton Hotels Corporation (HHC) of the USA and Hilton Hotels International, a subsidiary of Hilton plc which is based in the UK, were separated under different ownership in 1964, some 45 years after Conrad Hilton opened the first hotel to bear his surname in Chicago. Since that time the relationship between the two chains bearing the Hilton name has frequently been acrimonious and was never close until 1996 when both chains appointed chairmen committed to capitalising fully on the strength of the Hilton brand. Negotiations culminated in 1997 with an agreement to form a wide-ranging strategic alliance between the two chains, covering a joint reservations system (boosted by $100 million spending on new technology), the extension of HHC's loyalty rewards to Hilton International, the adoption of joint brand identities including a new logo and joint marketing campaigns. To operationalise the strategic alliance the management of the two chains meet four times a year (Nissé, 1998).

In the tour-operating sector, examples of strategic alliances are less common as the preferred strategic method. One example is provided by the British based tour operator MyTravel which entered into a significant strategic alliance with the world's largest cruise line, Carnival Cruises, in April 1996 whereby Carnival acquired 29.5% of Airtours' ordinary share capital. The relationship was discontinued in 2001. Another British based tour operator, First Choice, however, entered a strategic alliance with Royal Caribbean Cruise Lines (RCCL) in 2000 whereby RCCL acquired an equity stake in First Choice plc.

A Conceptualisation of the Collaborative Process for International Airlines

Figures 7.2 (Evans, 2001a) provides a conceptual model of the strategic management processes involved in the formation of strategic alliances using the airline sector as an example. It can be argued that a four-stage process takes place. The process involves first, the strategic analysis of the internal organisational and external environmental 'drivers' which act as the underlying motivating reasons for alliance formation. Second, alternative strategic options are postulated and evaluated and the option of strategic alliance formation (either with or without equity) participation is chosen. Third, implementation issues have to be considered including the choice of appropriate partners and issues relating to the structure and scope of the alliance. Finally, the strategic alliance is evaluated against selected criteria purporting to measure the success of the alliance. The evaluation of the alliance is fed back into the analytical phase so that any changes based upon experience can be incorporated.

Motivations for Strategic Alliance Formation

Identifying 'Driving' Forces

A number of studies have sought to identify the underlying motivations for the formation of strategic alliances (Glaister and Buckley, 1996; Bennett, 1997) and it is generally accepted that some types of external driver need to be present (Faulkner, 1995). Two well-known authors in this field (Child and Faulkner, 1998) have suggested that there may be six key external driving forces and four key internal needs acting as motivational forces in the formation of alliances.

External driving forces for alliance formation are:

1. Turbulence in world markets and high economic uncertainty.
2. The existence of economies of scale and/or scope as competitive cost-reducing agents.

3. The globalisation or regionalisation of a growing number of industries.

Poon (1993) referred to the a fourth pattern of related diversification as *diagonal diversification.* This form of diversification (common in service industries) utilises a common platform of information-utilising technology to target a group of customers with a closely related set of products. Thus, banks use their customer databases to target their customers with offers of insurance, mortgages, financial planning services and possibly travel products. In a similar way Saga, a UK company that developed travel products for the over-55 age categories, has more recently targetted its customers with a range of financial services. Another example would be provided by American Express, which is involved in travel related and financial services. Many of its sales in leisure travel are to its American Express credit card holders. Diagonal diversification offers the following benefits:

- It allows organisations to get close to their customers and lower costs for each product by sharing overheads across several product categories.
- It allows organisations to benefit from economies of scope and systems savings.
- It is cheaper for one organisation to produce a combination of services rather than for many organisations to produce each separately.

Diagonal diversification is illustrated in Figure 7.2.

Unrelated diversification (sometimes termed *conglomerate* diversification) carries greater risk than related diversification as it involves producing new products for markets with which the organisation is unfamiliar. Businesses tend to take this option when they see serious restrictions on growth potential in their existing markets, and in related markets, or when they see significant opportunities for growth in new market areas. In addition, there are potential economies of scale, opportunities to build on existing competences and the possibility of synergy.

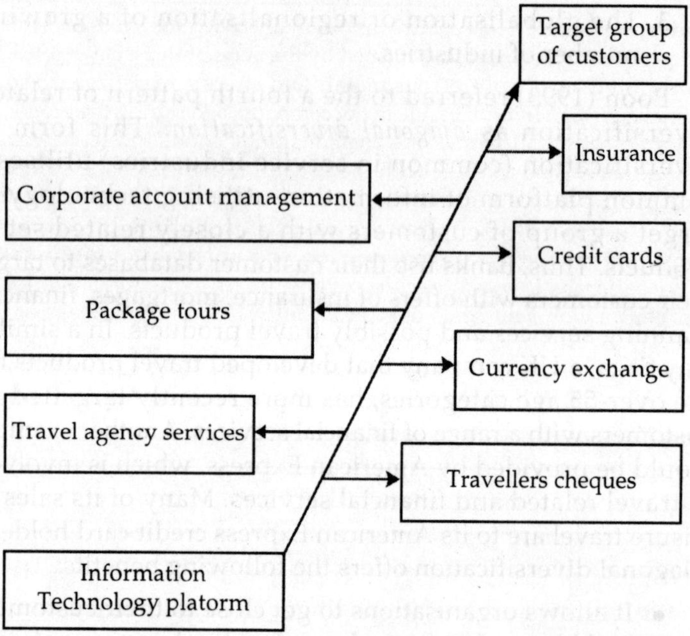

Figure 7.2: Diagonal diversification in travel and tourism.

Unrelated Diversification at Tui AG

Tui is a leading integrated tourism and services group. The tourism companies that are part of the Tui Group includes the German-based TUI Travel Group and the British-based Thomson Travel Group which are active in 15 European source markets. Familiar brand names to European travellers, such as TUI, Thomson Holidays and Fritidsresor, well-known travel agency chains such as FIRST, Holland International and Lunn Poly, and airlines Britannia and Hapag-Lloyd-Flug are all part of the Tui Group. Through strategic alliances with Nouvelles Frontiéres and Alpitour, the Group has also gained access to the French and Italian travel markets. The logistics and energy divisions complete the group's portfolio of activities. In the 1999/2000 financial year the group achieved a turnover of some 22 billion euros, 50 per cent of which was generated in the field of tourism. However, the group intends to increase this proportion amount to 80 per cent in future years.

Although Tui is now best known for its travel and tourism activities, this strategic focus represents a radical diversification away from its industrial roots. The company was originally called the Prussian Mining and Iron and Steel and was formed by the state of Prussian in 1923. In addition to coal, non-ferrous metals and energy, logistics also soon came to play an important role in the company, and during the economic boom of the 1950s and 1960s the consumer goods industry was of importance. Nevertheless, with the structural changes in the economy and the growing difficulties on the European raw and basic materials markets, Preussag as it was called was eventually confronted with the question of what future direction the company should take. Consequently, Preussag decided to give up its industrial activities to concentrate on new fields of growth. Since 1997 the entire face of the Group has changed. The companies now focus their attentions on the services sector, and with the acquisition and integration of TUI and Thomson Travel, particularly on the core business sector of tourism. The corporate name changed to Tui in 2002.

Stability Strategies (Maintain the Activities of the SBU)

An organisation's SBUs may choose stability over growth by continuing current activities without any significant change in direction. Stability strategies are not the same as 'doing nothing', for to remain stable actions have to be taken to defend the current market position from competitors. There may be several reasons for opting for such a strategic direction.

- The current environment is hostile or unpredictable making investment required for growth unattractive.
- A balance has to be maintained in the organisation so that finite resources have to be deployed in other SBUs which provide greater opportunities.
- A position of maturity has been reached where further growth is difficult and emphasis is placed on defending the current position.
- Many small business owners opt for this strategy as they are happy with their position having found a niche that they understand and which they are able to defend.

Stability strategies can be very useful in the short to medium term but can be dangerous in the longer-term as competitors start to make inroads into market share. The Thomson Travel Group (now a part of Tui AG), for example, was the market leader in the UK outbound holiday market from its entry to the market in 1965. It grew rapidly during the 1960s and 1970s and defended its market leadership position aggressively through discounting and other methods when necessary. However, its market share steadily decreased in the 1980s and early 1990s and Airtours (now MyTravel plc) was viewed as being consistently a step ahead of the UK number one (Bywater, 2001).

Wheelan and Hunger (2002) identified three variants of stability:

1. *Pause/proceed with caution* – is an opportunity to rest and reflect before continuing a growth or retrenchment strategy. It represents a deliberate attempt to make only incremental improvements until the environment changes. Such a strategy may be the result of excessive growth in the past, which has led to pressures on the organisation or from the need to stabilise after a period of decline.
2. *No change* – is a decision to do nothing new, choosing to continue current operations for the foreseeable future. Returns are adequate in the current position so why put these returns at risk by going after growth?
3. *Profit* – is a decision to do nothing new in a worsening environmental position but instead to act as though the organisation's problems are only temporary. The profit strategy attempts to support profits when an organisation's sales are declining by reducing investment and reducing unnecessary expenditure.

Retrenchment Strategies (Reduce the Activities of the SBU)

An organisation's SBU may pursue a retrenchment strategy when it is in a weak competitive position and the environment remains hostile for the alternative stability or growth strategies. For example, in the period following the 11th September, 2001 terrorist attacks in America, travel companies around the world chose to reduce the scale of their operations in response to the severe drop in demand. Aer Lingus, the Irish airline, for example, which relied on the Transatlantic trade (which was particularly badly hit) for about 70% of its revenues, scaled back a large parts of its operations in the wake of the attacks, looked for potential partners and sought additional sources of finance. Swissair and the Belgian airline Sabena both went bankrupt.

Wheelan and Hunger (2002) identified four variants of retrenchment:

1. *Turnaround* – emphasises the improvement in operational efficiency when an organisation has problems which whilst serious are not critical. Analogous to a weight reduction diet, Pearce and Robbins (1994) view such a strategy as a two-stage process involving contraction followed by consolidation. Contraction is the initial effort to 'stop the bleeding' with general cutbacks in size and costs followed by consolidation which implements a programme to stabilise the now leaner organisation.
2. *Captive company* – involves giving up independence in return for security whereby management offers the company to one of its largest customers to ensure survival. The customer guarantees the survival of the company by offering a long-term contract.
3. *Sell out/divestment* – if an organisation or SBU is in a weak competitive position it may choose to retrench through selling the entire organisation or divesting those SBUs that are in a weak position in order to provide finance for those that are stronger.
4. *Bankruptcy/liquidation* – occurs when the organisation finds itself in a very poor competitive position with few prospects. Bankruptcy (sometimes called administration) involves giving up the management of the company to the courts in return for some settlement of the corporation's obligations. The court appointed managers would attempt to keep the organisation going as a 'going concern'. By contrast liquidation is the termination of the organisation the organisation is

too weak to be sold to others as a going concern and any assets are sold in order to pay as much as possible to the organisation's creditors.

Strategic Development and Risk

There are risks associated with all forms of strategic development. The risks are smallest when development is largely based upon existing core competences and when it takes place in existing markets. The risks are greatest when development requires entry to unrelated markets. Whether or not the risks are worth taking will depend upon the current position of the organisation and the state of its markets and products. Entry to new markets, whether related or unrelated, will depend upon the business's assessment of the opportunities in new markets compared to opportunities in its existing markets.

BIBLIOGRAPHY

Ansoff, I. (1987) *Corporate Strategy*. London: Penguin.

Ambrosini, V., Johnson, G. and Scholes, K. (eds) (1998) *Exploring Techniques of Analysis and Evaluation in Strategic Management.*Harlow: Prentice Hall.

Archer, B.H. (1996) Economic Impact Analysis. *Annuals of Tourism Research*, 23(3), 704 – 7.

Argenti, J. (1965) *Corporate Planning*. London: Allen and Unwin.

Argyris, C. (1977) Double Loop Learning in Organisations. *Harvard Business Review*, September-October, pp. 115 – 125.

Argyris. C. (1992) *On Organisational Learning*. London: Blackwell.

Argyris, C. and Schon, D. (1978) *Organisation Learning: A Theory of Action Perspective*. Reading, MA: Addison Wesley.

Atkinson, H., Berry, A. and Jarvis, R. (1995) *Business Accounting for Hospitality and Tourism*. London: International Thomson Business Press.

Bartlett, C. and Ghoshal, S. (1987) Managing Across Borders: New Organisational Responses. *Sloan Management Review*, Fall, 45 – 53.

Bartlett, C. and Ghoshal, S. (1989) *Managing Across Borders: The Transnational Solution*. Cambridge, MA: Harvard Business School Press.

Baden-Fuller, C. and Stopford, J. (1992) *Rejuvenating the Mature Business*. Oxford: Routledge.

Barney, J.B. (2002) *Gaining and Sustaining Competitive Advantage*. Upper Saddle River, NJ: Prentice Hall.

Brown, D.O. and Kwansol. F.A. (1999) Using IRR and NPV Models to Evaluate Societal Costs of Tourism Projects in Developing Countries. *International Journal of Hospitality Management*, 18(1), 31 – 43.

Bull, A. (1995) *The Economics of Travel and Tourism*, 2nd edn. Melbourne: Longman.

Bywater, M. (2001) Who Owns Whom in the European Travel Distribution Industry, in D. Buhalis and E. Laws (eds), *Tourism*

Distribution Channels: Practices, Issues and Transformations. London: Continuum.

Campbell, A.J. and Verbeke, A. (1994) The Globalisation of Service Sector Multinationals. *Long Range Planning,* 27(2), 95 – 102.

Contractor, F. and Lorange, P. (1988) Why Should Firms Cooperate? The Strategy and Economic Basis for Cooperative Ventures. In F. Contractor and P. Lorange (eds), *Cooperative Strategies in International Business,* Lexington, MA: Lexington Books, 3 – 30.

Cravens, D.W., Greenley, G., Piercy, N.F. and Slater S. (1997) Integrating Contemporary Strategic Management Perspectives. *Long Range Planning,* 30 (4), August, 493 – 506.

Cronshaw, M., Davis, E. and Kay, J. (1990) On Being Stuck in the Middle or 'Good Food Costs Less at Sainsburys'. Working paper, *Centre for Business Strategy,* London School of Business.

Davidow, W.H. and Malone, M.S. (1992) *Structuring and Revitalising the Corporation for the 21st Century – The Virtual Corporation.* London: Harper Business.

Demarest, M. (1997) Understanding Knowledge Management. *Long Range Planning,* 30(3), 374 – 384.

Douglas, S.P. and Wind Y. (1987) The Myth of Globalisation. *Columbia Journal of World Business,* Winter, 19 – 29.

Doz., Y. (1986) *Strategic Management in Multinational Companies.* Oxford: Pergamon Press.

Doganis, R. (2001) *The Airline Business in the 21st Century.* London: Routledge.

Doran, R. (2000) EasyJet Plans Price War. *The Times,* London, p. 29.

Dyson, J.R. (2001) *Accounting for Non-Accounting Students,* 5th edn. Harlow: Pearson Education.

Ellis, J. and Williams, D. (1993) *Corporate Strategy and Financial Analysis.* London: Pitman.

Ellis J. and Williams, D. (1995) *International Business Strategy.* London: Pitman.

Finlay, P. (2000) *Strategic Management: An Introduction to Business and Corporate Strategy.* Harlow: Pearson Education.

French, T. (1998) The Future of Global Distribution Systems. *Travel and Tourism Analyst,* 3.

Glaister, K.W. and Buckley, P.J. (1996) Strategic Motives for International Alliance Formation. *Journal of Management Studies,* 33(3), 301 – 332.

Go, F. and Pine, R. (1995) *Globalisation Strategy in the Hotel Industry.* London: Routledge.

Go. F. (1996) A Conceptual Framework for Managing Global Tourism and Hospitality Marketing. *Tourism Recreation Research,* 21(2), 37 – 43.

Grant, R.M. (1991) The Resource Based Theory of Competitive Advantage: Implications for Strategy Formulation. *California Management Review,* 33 (Spring), 114 – 135.

Grant, R.M. (1997) The Knowledge-based View of the Firm: Implications for Management Practice. *Long Range Planning*, 30(3), 450 – 454.

Haberberg, A. and Rieple, A. (2001) *The Strategic Management of Organisations*. Harlow: Pearson Education.

Hamel, G. (1991) Competition for Competence and Inter-Partner Learning within International Strategic Alliances. *Strategic Management Journal*, 12 (Special Summer Issue), 83 – 104.

Hall, R. (1992) The Strategic Analysis of Intangible Resources, *Strategic Management Journal*, 13, 135 – 144.

Handy C.B. (1993) *Understanding Organisations*, 4th edn. London: Penguin.

Hamel, G. and Prahalad, C.K. (1985) Do Your Really Have a Global Strategy? *Harvard Business Review*, July / August.

Hamel, G., Doz, Y.L. and Prahalad, C.K. (1989) Collaborate with Your Competitors – and Win. *Harvard Business Review*, Jan / Feb, 133 – 139.

Hamel, G. and Prahalad, C.K. (1989) Strategic Intent. *Harvard Business Review*, 67(3), 63 – 76.

Hamel, G. and Prahalad, C.K. (1994) *Competing for the Future*. Cambridge, MA: Harvard Business School Press.

Hanlon, P. (1996) *Global Airlines: Competition in a Transnational Industry*. Oxford: Butter worth-Heinemann.

Hall, R. (1992) The Strategic Analysis of Intangible Resources. *Strategic Management Journal*, 13, 135 – 44.

Heskett, J.L., Sasser, W.F. and Schlesinger, L.A. (1997) *The Service Profit Chain*. New York: Simon and Schuster.

Heene, A. and Sanchez, R. (eds) (1997) *Competence-Based Strategic Management*. New York: John Wiley.

Henzler, H. and Rall, W. (1986) 'Facing Up to the Globalisation Challenge', *McKinsey Quarterly*, Winner.

Heene, A. and Sanchez, R. (eds) (1997) *Competence-based Strategic Management*. London: John Wiley.

Heracleous, L. (1998) Strategic Thinking or Strategic Planning. *Long Range Planning*, 30(3), 481 – 487.

Holloway, S. (1998) *Changing Planes: A Strategic Management Perspective on an Industry in Transition*. Aldershot: Ashgate.

Johnson, G. and Scholes, K. (2002) *Exploring Corporate Strategy*. Harlow: Pearson Education.

Johnson, G. (1987) *Strategic Change and the Management Process*. Oxford: Blackwell.

Johnson, G. and Scholes, K. (1998) *Exploring Corporate Strategy*, 5th edn. Hemel Hempstead: Prentice Hall.

Johnson, G. and Scholes, K. (1998) *Exploring Corporate Strategy*, 6th edn. Hemel Hempstead: Prentice Hall.

Kay, J. (1993) *Foundations of Corporate Success*. Oxford: Oxford University Press.

Kay, J. (1995) Learning to Define the Core Business. *Financial Times*, 1 December.

Keller, P. (1996) Globalisation and Tourism. *Globalisation and Tourism*, 38 Editions (AIEST). Switzerland: St Gallen.

Knowles, T., Diamantis, D. and El-Mourhabi, J.B. (2001) *The Globalisation of Tourism and Hospitality: A Strategic Perspective.* London: Continuum.

Kotas, R. and Conlan, M. (1997) *Hospitality Accounting*, 5th edn. London: International Thomson Business Press.

Kotler, P. (1997) *Marketing Management Analysis, Planning, Implementation and Control*, 9th edn. Englewood Cliffs, NJ: Prentice Hall International.

Lewin, K. (1947) Feedback Problems of Social Diagnosis and Action: Part II-B of Frontiers in Group Dynamics. *Human Relations*, 1, 147 – 153.

Lewin, K. (1951) *Field Theory in Social Science.* New York: Harper & Brothers.

Levitt, T. (1983) The Globalisation of Markets. *Harvard Business Review*, May/June.

Lenosky, T.J., Kress, J.D., Collins, L.A., Kwon, I. and McKiernan, P. (1997) Strategy Past; Strategy Futures. *Long Range Planning*, 30(5), 790 – 798.

Litteljohn, D. (1997) Hotel Chains and Their Strategic Appraisal, in M. Foley, J. Lennon and G. Maxwell (eds), *Hospitality, Tourism and Leisure Management.* London: Cassell.

Lynch, R. (2000) *Corporate Strategy*, 2nd edn. Harlow: Pearson Education.

Mathieson, A. and Wall, G. (1982) *Tourism: Economic, Physical and Social Impacts.* London and New York: Longman.

Miles, R.E. and Snow, C.C. (1978) *Organisational Strategy, Structure and Process.* New York: McGraw-Hill.

Mintzberg, H., Quinn, J.B. and Ghoshal, S. (1995) *The Strategy Process: Concepts, Contexts and Cases, European Edition.* Englewood Cliffs, NJ: Prentice Hall.

Mintzberg, H. (1987) Crafting Strategy. *Harvard Business Review*, July – August.

Mintzberg, H. (1991) *The Strategy Process – Concepts, Contexts, Cases.* Englewood Cliffs, NJ: Prentice Hall.

Miller, D. (1992) The Generic Strategy Trap. *Journal of Business Strategy*, 13(1), 37 – 42.

Moss Kanter, R. (1989) *The Change Masters: Innovation and Entrepreneurship in the American Corporation.* Englewood Cliffs, NJ: Simon & Schuster.

Mules, T. (2000) Globalisation and the Economic Impacts of Tourism, in B. Faulkner, G. Moscardo and E. Laws (eds), *Tourism in the 21st Century: Lessons from Experience.* London: Continuum.

Mules, T. (2001) Globalisation and the Economic Impacts of Tourism, in B. Faulkner, G. Moscardo and E. Laws (eds), *Tourism in the 21st Century: Lessons from Experience.* London: Continuum.

Nickson, D. (1997) Continuity or Change in the International Hotel Industry, in M. Foley, J. Lennon and G. Maxwell (eds), *Hospitality, Tourism and Leisure Management*. London: Cassell.

Ohmae, K. (1989) The Global Logic of Strategic Alliances. *Harvard Business Review*, March/April, 143 – 154.

Ohmae, K. (1989) Managing in a Borderless World. *Harvard Business Review*, May/June, 152 – 161.

Owen G. (1998) *Accounting for Hospitality Tourism and Leisure*, 2nd edn. Harlow: Longman.

Pettigrew, A.M. (1988) *The Management of Strategic Change*. Oxford: Blackwell.

Pearce II, J.A. and Robbins, D.K. (1994) Retrenchment Remains the Foundation of Business Turnaround. *Strategic Management Journal*, June, 313 – 323.

Penrose, E. (1959) *The Theory of the Growth of the Firm*. Oxford: Oxford University Press.

Porter, M.E. (1985) *Competitive Advantage*. New York: Free Press.

Porter, M.E. (1980) *Competitive Strategy: Techniques for Analysing Industries and Competitors*. New York: Free Press.

Porter, M.E. (1986a) *Competition in Global Business*. Cambridge, MA: Harvard University Press.

Porter M.E. (1986b) Changing Patterns of International Competition. *California Management Review*, 28(2), 9 – 40.

Porter, M.E. (1990) *The Competitive Advantage of Nations*. New York: Free Press.

Poon, A. (1993) *Tourism, Technology and Competitive Strategies*. Wallingford: CABI.

Prahalad, C.K. and Doz, Y.L. (1987) *The Multinational Mission: Balancing Local Demands and Global Vision*. New York: Free Press.

Prahalad, C.K. and Hamel, G. (1990) The Core Competence of the Organisation. *Harvard Business Review*, 90, 79 – 91.

Prahalad, C.K. and Hamel, G. (1990) The Core Competence of the Corporation, in *Harvard Business Review*, reprinted in Segal-Horn, S. (1998) (ed.), *The Stretegy Reader*. Oxford: Blackwell in Association with The Open University.

Quinn, J.B. and Voyer, J. (1998) Logical Incrementalism: Managing Strategy Formation, in H. Mintzberg, J.B. Quinn and S. Ghoshal (eds), *The Strategy Process*. Englewood Cliffs, NJ: Prentice Hall.

Quinn, J.B. (1980) Managing Strategic Change. *Sloan Management Review*, Summer 1980, 3 – 20.

Quinn, J.B. (1980) *Strategies for Change*. Homewood, JL: Irwin.

Quinn, J.B. (1978) Strategic Change; Logical Incrementalism. *Sloan Management Review*, Fall.

Quinn, J.B. (1992) *The Intelligent Enterprise*. New York: The Free Press.

Quinn, J.B. and Voyer, J. (1994) *The Strategy Process*. Englewood Cliffs, NJ: Prentice Hall.

Quinn, J.B., Doorley, T. and Paquette, P. (1990) Technology in Services: Rethinking Strategic Focus. *Sloan Management Review*, 31(2), 79 – 87.

Reeve, T. (1990) The Firm as a Nexus of Internal and External Contracts, in M. Aoki, M. Gustafsson and O.E. Williamson (eds), *The Firm as a Nexus of Treaties*. London: Sage.

Rumelt, R. (1991) How Much Does Industry Matter? *Strategic Management Journal*, 12, 167 – 185.

Rumelt, R. (1980) The Evaluation of Business Strategy, in W.F. Glueck, *Business Policy and Strategic Management*. New York: McGraw Hill.

Sanchez, R. and Heene, A. (eds) (1997) *Strategic Learning and Knowledge Management*. New York: Wiley.

Schein, E.H. (1985) Organisational Culture and Leadership. San Francisco: Jossey – Bass.

Sessa, R. (1996) Tourism Production, Tourism Products. *Globalisation and Tourism*, 38 (Editions AIEST). Switzerland: St Gallen.

Senge, P. (1990) The Leader's New Work: Building Learning Organisations. *Sloan Management Review*, 32(1), 7 – 22.

Smeral, E. (1996) Globalisation and Changes in the Competitiveness of Tourism Destinations, in *Globalisation and Tourism*, 38 (Editions AIEST). Switzerland: St Gallen.

Smeral, E. (1998) The Impact of Globalisation on Small and Medium Enterprises: New Challenges for Tourism Policies in European Countries. *Tourism Management*, 19(4), 371 – 380.

Stacey, R.D. (1993) *Strategic Management and Organisational Dynamics*. London: Pitman.

Stonehouse, G.H, Hamill, J., Campbell, D. and Purdie, A. (1999) *Global and Transnational Business – Strategy and Management*. London: John Wiley.

Stalk, G., Evans, P. and Shulmann, L.E. (1992) Competing on Capabilities: The New Rules of Corporate Strategy. *Harvard Business Review*, March/April, 57 – 69.

Tushman, M.L. and O'Reilly, C.A. (1996) *Winning Through Innovation: A Practical Guide to Leading Organisational Change and Renewal*. Boston, MA: Harvard Business School Press.

Vogel, H.L. (2001) *Travel Industry Economics*. Cambridge: Cambridge University Press.

Wager, J.E. (1997) Estimating the Economic Impacts of Tourism. *Annals of Tourism Reseach*, 24(3), 592 – 608.

Wahab, S. and Cooper, C. (2001) *Tourism in the Age of Globalisation*. London: Routledge.

Wheelen, T.S. and Hunger, J.D. (2002) *Strategic Management and Business Policy*, 8th edn. Upper Saddle River, NJ: Prentice Hall.

Williams, A. and Giardina, E. (1993) *Efficiency in the Public Sector: The Theory and Practice of Cost-Benefit Analysis.* London: Edward Elgar.
Williamson, O. (1975) *Markets and Hierarchies.* New York: Free Press.
World Tourism Organisation (1994) *Aviation and Tourism Policies: Balancing the Benefits.* London: Routledge.
w.w.w.compass-group.co.uk
w.w.w.cruise2.com
w.w.w.holidaybreak.com
Yip, G.S. (1992) *Total Global Strategy – Managing for Worldwide Competitive Advantage.* Englewood Cliffs, NJ: Prentice Hall.